EVOLVE

STUDENT'S BOOK

Leslie Anne Hendra, Mark Ibbotson,
and Kathryn O'Dell

1B

CAMBRIDGE
UNIVERSITY PRESS

CAMBRIDGE
UNIVERSITY PRESS

University Printing House, Cambridge CB2 8BS, United Kingdom

One Liberty Plaza, 20th Floor, New York, NY 10006, USA

477 Williamstown Road, Port Melbourne, VIC 3207, Australia

314–321, 3rd Floor, Plot 3, Splendor Forum, Jasola District Centre, New Delhi – 110025, India

79 Anson Road, #06–04/06, Singapore 079906

Cambridge University Press is part of the University of Cambridge.

It furthers the University's mission by disseminating knowledge in the pursuit of education, learning, and research at the highest international levels of excellence.

www.cambridge.org
Information on this title: www.cambridge.org/9781108414104

© Cambridge University Press 2019

First published 2019

20 19 18 17 16 15 14 13 12 11 10 9 8 7 6 5 4 3 2 1

Printed in Dubai by Oriental Press

A catalogue record for this publication is available from the British Library

ISBN 978-1-108-40521-8 Student's Book
ISBN 978-1-108-40503-4 Student's Book A
ISBN 978-1-108-40914-8 Student's Book B
ISBN 978-1-108-40522-5 Student's Book with Practice Extra
ISBN 978-1-108-40504-1 Student's Book with Practice Extra A
ISBN 978-1-108-40915-5 Student's Book with Practice Extra B
ISBN 978-1-108-40894-3 Workbook with Audio
ISBN 978-1-108-40859-2 Workbook with Audio A
ISBN 978-1-108-41191-2 Workbook with Audio B
ISBN 978-1-108-40512-6 Teacher's Edition with Test Generator
ISBN 978-1-108-41062-5 Presentation Plus
ISBN 978-1-108-41201-8 Class Audio CDs
ISBN 978-1-108-40791-5 Video Resource Book with DVD
ISBN 978-1-108-41200-1 Full Contact with DVD
ISBN 978-1-108-41152-3 Full Contact with DVD A
ISBN 978-1-108-41410-4 Full Contact with DVD B

Additional resources for this publication at www.cambridge.org/evolve

ACKNOWLEDGMENTS

The *Evolve* publishers would like to thank the following individuals and institutions who have contributed their time and insights into the development of the course:

Ivanova Monteros A., **Universidad Tecnológica Equinoccial (UTE)**, Ecuador; Monica Frenzel, **Universidad Andrés Bello**, Chile; Antonio Machuca Montalvo, **Organización The Institute TITUELS**, **Veracruz**, Mexico; Daniel Martin, **CELLEP**, Brazil; Roberta Freitas, **IBEU**, Brazil; Verónica Nolivos Arellano, Language Coordinator, Quito, Ecuador; Daniel Lowe, **Lowe English Services**, Panama; Maria Araceli Hernández Tovar, **Instituto Tecnológico Superior de San Luis Potosí**, Capital, Mexico; Lenise Butler, **Laureate**, Mexico; Gloria González Meza, **Instituto Politecnico Nacional, ESCA (University)**, Mexico; Miguel Ángel López, **Universidad Europea de Madrid**, Spain; Diego Ribeiro Santos, **Universidade Anhembi Morumbi**, São Paulo, Brazil; Esther Carolina Eueda Garcia, **UNITEC (Universidad Tecnologica Centroamericana)**, Honduras.

To our student cast, who have contributed their ideas and their time, and who appear throughout this book:

Anderson Batista, Brazil; Carolina Nascimento Negrão, Brazil; Felipe Martinez Lopez, Mexico; Jee-Hyo Moon, South Korea ; Jinny Lara, Honduras; Josue Lozano, Honduras; Julieth C. Moreno Delgado, Colombia; Larissa Castro, Honduras.

And special thanks to Katy Simpson, teacher and writer at *myenglishvoice.com*; and Raquel Ribeiro dos Santos, EFL teacher, EdTech researcher, blogger, and lecturer.

Authors' Acknowledgments:

The authors would like to extend their warmest thanks to all of the team at Cambridge University Press who were involved in creating this course. In particular, they would like to thank Ruby Davies and Robert Williams for their kindness, enthusiasm, and encouragement throughout the writing of the A1 level. They would also like to express their appreciation to Caroline Thiriau, whose understanding and support have been of great value. And they would like to thank Katie La Storia for her dedication and enthusiasm throughout the project.

Kathryn O'Dell would like to thank her parents (and grandparents) for passing down a love for words and stories. She also thanks her husband, Kevin Hurdman, for his loving support.

Leslie Anne Hendra would like to thank Michael Stuart Clark, her *sine qua non*, for his support and encouragement during this and other projects.

Mark Ibbotson would like to thank Aimy and Tom for their patience and understanding as family life was bent and squeezed around the project, and – especially – Nathalie, whose energy and creative solutions made it all possible.

The authors and publishers acknowledge the following sources of copyright material and are grateful for the permissions granted. While every effort has been made, it has not always been possible to identify the sources of all the material used, or to trace all copyright holders. If any omissions are brought to our notice, we will be happy to include the appropriate acknowledgements on reprinting and in the next update to the digital edition, as applicable.

Photo:

Key: B = Below, BG = Background, BL = Below Left, BR = Below Right, C = Centre, CL = Centre Left, CR = Centre Right, L = Left, R = Right, TC = Top Centre, TL = Top Left, TR = Top Right.

All images are sourced from Getty Images.

p. xvi (listen): Tara Moore/DigitalVision; p. xvi (say): Tara Moore/The Image Bank; p. xvi (write): Kohei Hara/DigitalVision; p. xvi (watch): Felbert+Eickenberg/Stock4B; p. xvi (students), p. 124: Klaus Vedfelt/DigitalVision; p. 106 (C): Hero Images; p. 66 (photo 5), p. 68 (2d, 2f, 2i), p. 82 (TC), p. 88, p. 117, p. 120 (fish), p. xvi (read): Westend61; p. 74: Caiaimage/Sam Edwards; p. 98 (walk): Alistair Berg/DigitalVision; p. 74, 84, 94, 106, 116, 126: Tom Merton/Caiaimage; p. 80, p. 114 (woman): Tetra Images; p. 84 (soccer): Hinterhaus Productions/DigitalVision; p. 108 (book): PeopleImages/DigitalVision; p.66 (photo 2), p. 72 (cat), p. 118 (bread): Dorling Kindersley; p. 72 (cat), p. 118 (tomato): Dave King/Dorling Kindersleyl; p. 65: jameslee999/Vetta; p. 66 (photo 1): Phil Boorman/The Image Bank; p. 66 (photo 3): Vincent Besnault/The Image Bank; p. 66 (photo 4): David Zach/Stone; p. 66 (photo 6): LM Productions/Photodisc; p. 67: Jonathan Knowles/The Image Bank; p. 68 (2a, 2b): alvarez/E+; p. 68 (2c): Samuelsson, Kristofer; p. 68 (2e): Plume Creative/DigitalVision; p. 68 (2g): Jordan Siemens/Taxi; p. 68 (2h): Ezra Bailey/Taxi; p. 69: Lorentz Gullachsen/The Image Bank; p. 70 (BL): Robert Kneschke/EyeEm; p. 70 (BG), p. 108 (beautiful): Dougal Waters/DigitalVision; p. 71: Flavio Edreira/EyeEm; p. 72: Lane Oatey/Blue Jean Images; p. 73: Dave Nagel/Taxi; p. 75: Mint Images RF; p. 76 (surf): Christian Kober/AWL Images; p. 76 (skateboard): yanik88/iStock/Getty Images Plus; p. 76 (snowboarding): Maximilian Groß/EyeEm; p. 76 (draw): Ruth Jenkinson/Dorling Kindersley; p. 76 (boys): Resolution Productions/Blend Images; p. 76 (paint): Glowimages; p. 76 (sing): Kyle Monk/Blend Images; p. 76 9(dance): catalinere/iStock/Getty Images Plus; p. 76 (guitar): Justin Case/Taxi; p. 76 (swim): pixdeluxe/E+; p. 76 (wheel): Philip Gatward/Dorling Kindersley; p. 76 (CR), p. 121: Jose Luis Pelaez Inc/Blend Images; p. 77: Lilly Roadstones/The Image Bank; p. 78: Reza Estakhrian/Iconica; p. 79: PeopleImages/E+; p. 81: Allison Michael Orenstein/The Image Bank; p. 82 (TL): Kristy-Anne Glubish; p. 82 (TR): PhonlamaiPhoto/iStock/Getty Images Plus; p. 84 (photo 1): ibrahimaslann/iStock Editorial/Getty Images Plus; p. 84 (photo 2), p. xvi (teacher): Marc Romanelli/Blend Images; p. 84 (photo 3): Yew! Images/Image Source; p. 84 (photo 4): PaulBiryukov/iStock/Getty Images Plus; p. 85: Johannes Spahn/EyeEm; p. 86 (airplane): Jan Stromme/The Image Bank; p. 86 (woman): Caroline Schiff/Taxi; p. 86 (girl): Peathegee Inc/Blend Images; p. 86 (country): Instants/E+; p. 86 (parrot): Busakorn Pongparnit/Moment; p. 86 (boat): Richard Cummins/Lonely Planet Images; p. 86 (park): Lidija Kamansky/Moment Open; p. 87 (C): Waring Abbott/Michael Ochs Archives; p. 87 (hikers): Debra Brash/Perspectives; p. 87 (Lake): Jeff Greenberg/Universal Images Group; p. 89: Cláudio Policarpo/EyeEm; p. 90: Image Source; p. 92: Anna Gorin/Moment; p. 93: hadynyah/E+; p. 94 (Jim): John Lund/Marc Romanelli/Blend Images; p. 93 (Flo): Blend Images - Erik Isakson/Brand X Pictures; p. 94 (Carter): Alexander Robinson/Blend Images; p. 97: Darryl Leniuk/DigitalVision; p. 98 (TL): Chan Srithaweeporn/Moment; p. 98 (art): Randy Faris/Corbis/VCG; p. 98 (dinner, shopping): Cultura RM Exclusive/Frank and Helena; p. 98 (airport): Maskot; p. 98 (picnic): Uwe Krejci/DigitalVision; p. 99: Billy Hustace/Corbis Documentary; p. 100 (fall): Shobeir Ansari/Moment; p. 100 (summer): AL Hedderly/Moment; p. 100 (spring): Lelia Valduga; p. 100 (rainy): Chalabala/iStock/Getty Images Plus; p. 100 (dry): skodonnell/E+; p. 101: Julia Davila-Lampe/Moment; p. 102: Caiaimage/Chris Ryan; p. 103: filadendron/E+; p. 104: Rudimencial/iStock/Getty Images Plus; p. 105: ©Leonardo Muniz/Moment; 106 (TL): Toshi Sasaki/Photodisc; p. 106 (TC): skynesher/iStock/Getty Images Plus; p. 106 (TR): AJ_Watt/E+; p. 106 (CL): Luke Stettner/Photonica; p. 106 (CR): Mike Kemp/Blend Images; p. 107: Shanina/iStock/Getty Images Plus; p. 107 (TR): Simon Winnall/Taxi; p. 108 (kart): Images Of Our Lives/Archive Photos; p.108 (awful): PM Images/Stone; p. 108 (dog): Kevin Kozicki/Image Source; p. 108 (baby, quiet baby): Emma Kim/Cultura; p. 108 (fast car): Martin Barraud/Caiaimage; p. 108 (slow car): Michael Mrozek/EyeEm; p. 108 (shoe): Jeffrey Coolidge/The Image Bank; p. 108 (vacation): swissmediavision/E+; p. 109: Satoshi Yamada/EyeEm; p. 110: NexTser/iStock/Getty Images Plus; p. 111: real444/E+; p. 112: Mark Cuthbert/UK Press; p. 113: Mike Powell/Stone; p. 114 (toy car): Peter Zander/Photolibrary; p. 114 (shoe): Willer Amorim/EyeEm; 114 (comic): Bernd Vogel/Corbis; p. 115: George Steinmetz/Corbis Documentary; p. 116: Shan Shui/DigitalVision; p. 118 (chicken): Floortje/E+; p. 118 (coconut): RedHelga/E+; p. 118 (pineapple): Moodboard Stock Photography Ltd./Canopy; p. 118 (apple): t_kimura/E+; p. 118 (soup): David Marsden/Photolibrary; p. 118 (butter): SvetlanaK/iStock/Getty Images Plus; p. 118 (banana): Andy Crawford/Dorling Kindersley; p. 118 (cheese): Steven Mark Needham/Corbis Documentary; p. 118 (potato): jerryhat/E+; p. 114 (beef): Frank Bean/UpperCut Images; p. 118 (sandwich), p. 125: LauriPatterson/E+; p. 118 (orange): julichka/E+; p. 118 (lamb): pmphoto/iStock/Getty Images Plus; p. 118 (crackers): Bernard Prost/StockFood Creative; p. 118 (CR): Stephanie Leong/EyeEm; p. 119: Lumina Images/Blend Images; p. 120 (steak): Joy Skipper/Photolibrary; p. 120 (pizza): Nomadsoul1/iStock/Getty Images Plus; p. 120 (beans): Angela Bragato/EyeEm; p. 120 (chocolate): Angela Bragato/EyeEm; p. 120 (cookies): DigiPub/Moment; p. 120 (water): Retno Ayu Adiati/EyeEm; p. 122: Justin Case/The Image Bank; p. 123: Maarten De Beer/EyeEm; p.124 (Chinese): Naltik/iStock/Getty Images Plus; p. 124 (Mexican): rez-art/iStock/Getty Images Plus; p. 124 (Italian): Jon Spaull/Perspectives; p. 126: andresr/E+.

The following images are sourced from other libraries:

p. 76 (music): otnaydur/Shutterstock; p. 84 (CR): AlanHaynes.com/Alamy Stock Photo.

Front cover photography by Arctic-Images/The Image Bank/Getty Images.

Illustrations by: Joanna Kerr (New Division) p. 100; Dusan Lakicevic (Beehive Illustration) pp. 88, 90, 91.

Audio production by CityVox, New York.

EVOLVE

SPEAKING MATTERS

EVOLVE is a six-level American English course for adults and young adults, taking students from beginner to advanced levels (CEFR A1 to C1).

Drawing on insights from language teaching experts and real students, EVOLVE is a general English course that gets students speaking with confidence.

This student-centered course covers all skills and focuses on the most effective and efficient ways to make progress in English.

Confidence in teaching.
Joy in learning.

Better Learning WITH EVOLVE

Better Learning is our simple approach where insights we've gained from research have helped shape content that drives results. Language evolves, and so does the way we learn. This course takes a flexible, student-centered approach to English language teaching.

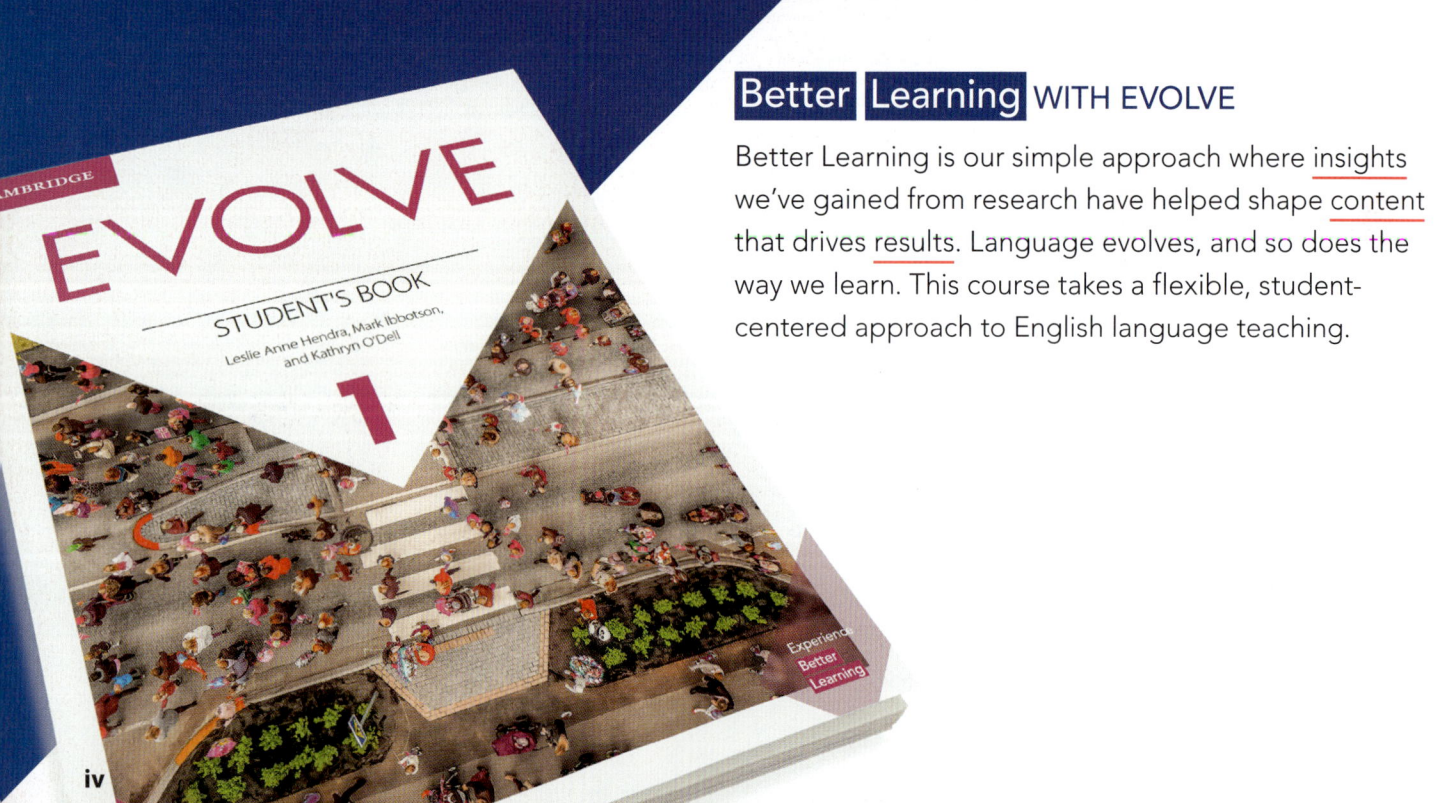

EVOLVE
STUDENT'S BOOK
Leslie Anne Hendra, Mark Ibbotson, and Kathryn O'Dell
1

Meet our student contributors

Videos and ideas from real students feature throughout the Student's Book.

Our student contributors describe themselves in three words.

LARISSA CASTRO

Friendly, honest, happy
Centro Universitario
Tecnológico, Honduras

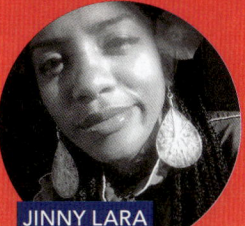

JINNY LARA

Free your mind
Centro Universitario
Tecnológico, Honduras

CAROLINA NASCIMENTO NEGRÃO

Nice, determined, hard-working
Universidade Anhembi Morumbi,
Brazil

JOSUE LOZANO

Enthusiastic, cheerful, decisive
Centro Universitario
Tecnológico, Honduras

JULIETH C. MORENO DELGADO

Decisive, reliable, creative
Fundación Universitaria
Monserrate, Colombia

ANDERSON BATISTA

Resilient, happy, dreamer
Universidade Anhembi
Morumbi, Brazil

FELIPE MARTINEZ LOPEZ

Reliable, intrepid, sensitive
Universidad del Valle de
México, Mexico

JEE-HYO MOON (JUNE)

Organized, passionate, diligent
Mission College, USA

Student-generated content

EVOLVE is the first course of its kind to feature real student-generated content. We spoke to over 2,000 students from all over the world about the topics they would like to discuss in English and in what situations they would like to be able to speak more confidently.

The ideas are included throughout the Student's Book and the students appear in short videos responding to discussion questions.

INSIGHT

Research shows that achievable speaking role models can be a powerful motivator.

CONTENT

Bite-sized videos feature students talking about topics in the Student's Book.

RESULT

Students are motivated to speak and share their ideas.

"It's important to provide learners with interesting or stimulating topics."

Teacher, Mexico (Global Teacher Survey, 2017)

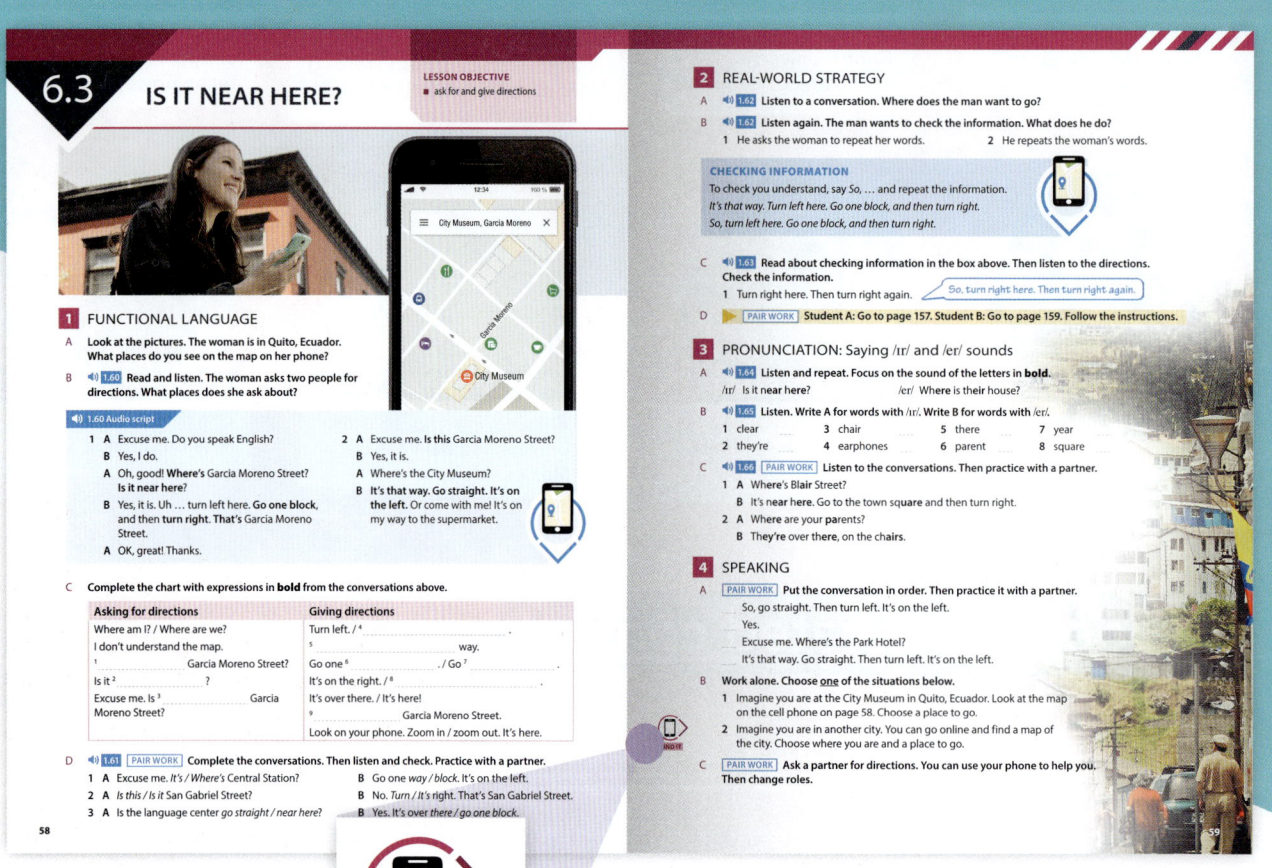

Find it

FIND IT

INSIGHT
Research with hundreds of teachers and students across the globe revealed a desire to expand the classroom and bring the real world in.

CONTENT
Find it are smartphone activities that allow students to bring live content into the class and personalize the learning experience with research and group activities.

RESULT
Students engage in the lesson because it is meaningful to them.

Designed for success

Pronunciation

INSIGHT
Research shows that only certain aspects of pronunciation actually affect comprehensibility and inhibit communication.

CONTENT
EVOLVE focuses on the aspects of pronunciation that most affect communication.

RESULT
Students understand more when listening and can be clearly understood when they speak.

Register check

INSIGHT
Teachers report that their students often struggle to master the differences between written and spoken English.

CONTENT
Register check draws on research into the Cambridge English Corpus and highlights potential problem areas for learners.

RESULT
Students transition confidently between written and spoken English and recognize different levels of formality as well as when to use them appropriately.

6.1 GOOD PLACES

LESSON OBJECTIVE
- talk about places in the city

1 LANGUAGE IN CONTEXT

A ◀)) 1.57 Lucas and Robert are in New York City. Read and listen to their conversation. Where is Lucas from? Where is Robert from? What does Lucas want to do on Saturday?

B ◀)) 1.57 Read and listen again. Are the sentences true or false?
1 Lucas has a lot of time in New York City.   2 There is no restaurant in the hotel.

◀)) 1.57 Audio script

GLOSSARY
neighborhood (n) an area of a city

Lucas I'm here, in New York City, for a week. And then I go home to Paris on Sunday.
Robert So you don't have a lot of time to see my great city.
Lucas No, I don't. There's no free time this week – it's work, work, work! But I have some time on Saturday.
Robert OK. There are a lot of places to see and things to do on the weekend. Where is your **hotel**?
Lucas It's near Central Park.
Robert No way! Central Park is great. There are some interesting museums near the **park**. Oh, and there's a **zoo** in the park!
Lucas Cool! What about places to eat? There's no **restaurant** in my hotel.
Robert Hmm … for breakfast, there's a nice **café** near here. And there are a lot of great restaurants in this neighborhood, too.
Lucas Great. Do you know some good **stores**? I don't have a lot of free time, but …
Robert Oh, yeah. There are a lot of great stores in New York. So … no museum, no park, no zoo – just shopping?
Lucas Yes!

INSIDER ENGLISH
Use *No way!* to show surprise.
No way! Central Park is great.

2 VOCABULARY: Places in cities

A ◀)) 1.58 Listen and repeat the words.

bookstore · hospital · movie theater · restaurant · supermarket
café · hotel · museum · school · zoo
college · mall · park · store

B ▶ Now do the vocabulary exercises for 6.1 on page 145.

C PAIR WORK Which three places in cities do you both like? Which three don't you like?

54

3 GRAMMAR: *There's, There are; a lot of, some, no*

A Circle the correct answers. Use the sentences in the grammar box to help you.
1 Use *There's* with singular / plural nouns.
2 Use *There are* with singular / plural nouns.
3 Use *an / no* in negative sentences.
4 Use *some* for exact numbers / when you don't know how many things there are.

There's (= There is), There are; a lot of, some, no

There's no free time this week.	**There are** some interesting museums near the park.	**no** = zero
There's a zoo in the park.	**There are** a lot of good places to see on the weekend.	**a/an** = one
There's a nice café near here.		**some** = a small number
		a lot of = a large number

B Circle the correct words to complete the sentences.
1 *There's / There are* a lot of stores in the mall.
2 *There's / There are* a supermarket near the college.
3 There are *a / some* good cafés on Boston Road.
4 There's *a / a lot of* big hospital in the city.
5 There are *a lot of / no* stores, so it's great for shopping.
6 In my city, there are *a / no* zoos.

C ▶ Now go to page 134. Look at the grammar chart and do the grammar exercise for 6.1.

D Write sentences about your city. Use *there is/there are*, *a/an*, *some*, *a lot of*, and *no*. Then check your accuracy.
There's _____ .
There's _____ .
There are _____ .
There are _____ .
There is/are no _____ .

ACCURACY CHECK
Use *there are*, not *there is*, before *a lot of* and *some* + plural noun.
There is some museums in this city. ✗
There are some museums in this city. ✓

E PAIR WORK Compare your sentences with a partner.

4 SPEAKING

PAIR WORK Talk about the things in your neighborhood. Then compare with a partner. What's the same? What's different?

There are some good restaurants near my home.
Same! And there's a movie theater near my home.

55

Accuracy check

ACCURACY CHECK
Use *there are*, **not** *there is*, before *a lot of* and *some* + plural noun.
There is some museums in this city. ✗
There are some museums in this city. ✓

INSIGHT
Some common errors can become fossilized if not addressed early on in the learning process.

CONTENT
Accuracy check highlights common learner errors (based on unique research into the Cambridge Learner Corpus) and can be used for self-editing.

RESULT
Students avoid common errors in their written and spoken English.

"The presentation is very clear and there are plenty of opportunities for student practice and production."

Jason Williams, Teacher, Notre Dame Seishin University, Japan

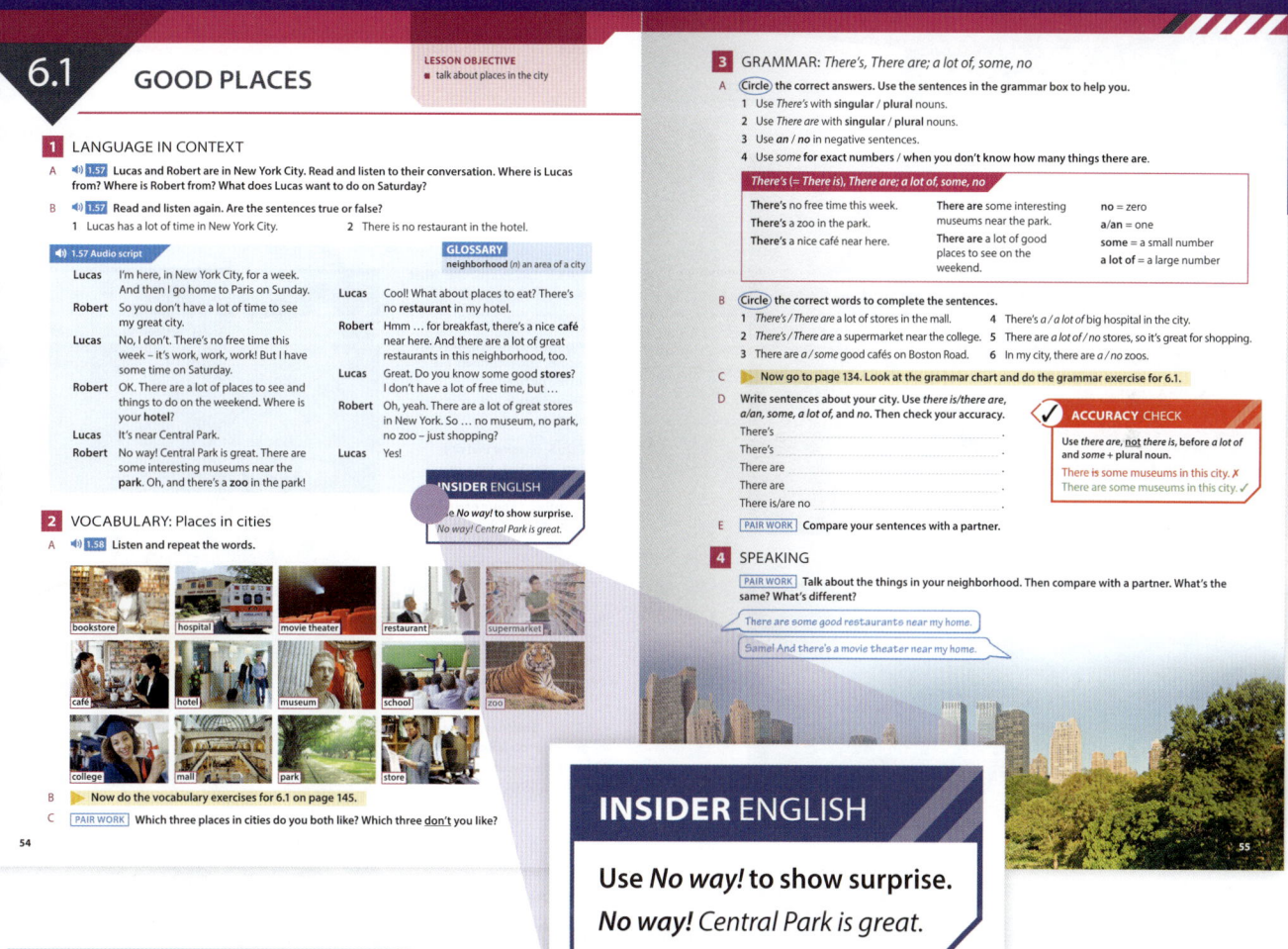

Insider English

INSIGHT

Even in a short exchange, idiomatic language can inhibit understanding.

CONTENT

Insider English focuses on the informal language and colloquial expressions frequently found in everyday situations.

RESULT

Students are confident in the real world.

You spoke. We listened.

Students told us that speaking is the most important skill for them to master, while teachers told us that finding speaking activities which engage their students and work in the classroom can be challenging.

That's why EVOLVE has a whole lesson dedicated to speaking: Lesson 5, *Time to speak*.

Time to speak

INSIGHT

Speaking ability is how students most commonly measure their own progress, but is also the area where they feel most insecure. To be able to fully exploit speaking opportunities in the classroom, students need a safe speaking environment where they can feel confident, supported, and able to experiment with language.

CONTENT

Time to Speak is a unique lesson dedicated to developing speaking skills and is based around immersive tasks which involve information sharing and decision making.

RESULT

Time to speak lessons create a buzz in the classroom where speaking can really thrive, evolve, and take off, resulting in more confident speakers of English.

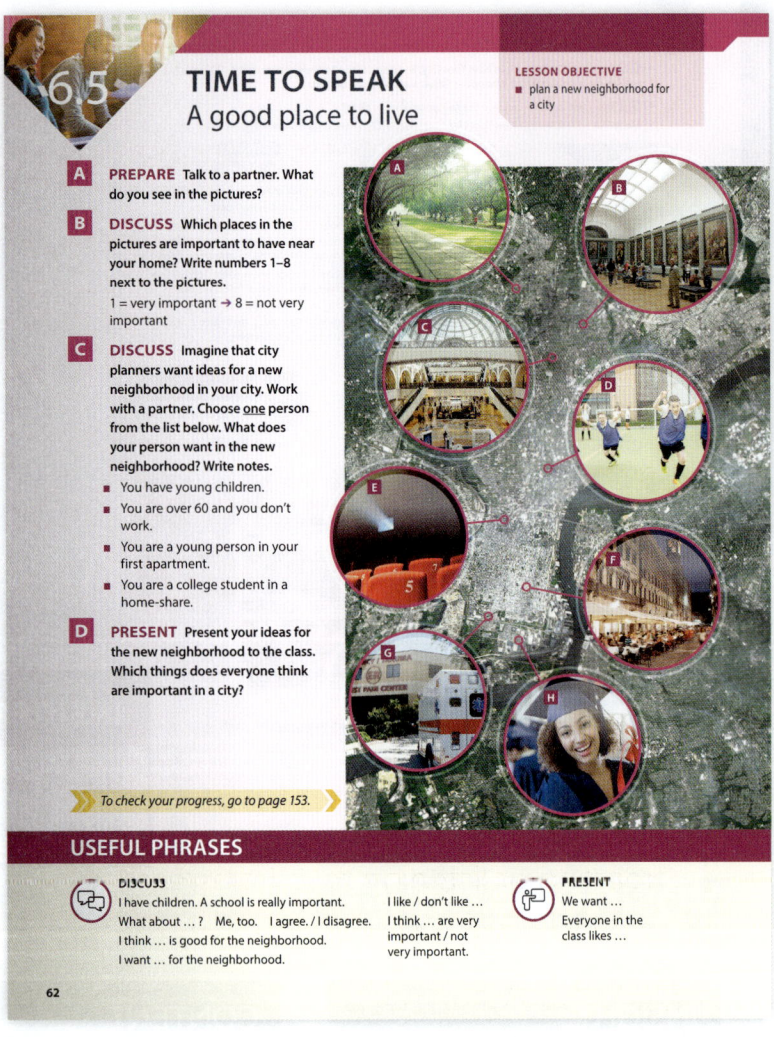

Experience Better Learning with EVOLVE: a course that helps both teachers and students on every step of the language learning journey.

Speaking matters. Find out more about creating safe speaking environments in the classroom.

EVOLVE unit structure

Unit opening page

Each unit opening page activates prior knowledge and vocabulary and immediately gets students speaking.

Lessons 1 and 2

These lessons present and practice the unit vocabulary and grammar in context, helping students discover language rules for themselves. Students then have the opportunity to use this language in well-scaffolded, personalized speaking tasks.

Lesson 3

This lesson is built around a functional language dialogue that models and contextualizes useful fixed expressions for managing a particular situation. This is a real world strategy to help students handle unexpected conversational turns.

Lesson 4

This is a combined skills lesson based around an engaging reading or listening text. Each lesson asks students to think critically and ends with a practical writing task.

Lesson 5

Time to speak is an entire lesson dedicated to developing speaking skills. Students work on collaborative, immersive tasks which involve information sharing and decision making.

CONTENTS

Functional language	Listening	Reading	Writing	Speaking
■ Answer the phone and greet people; ask how things are going **Real-world strategy** ■ React to news		**Jamie's blog** ■ A blog about a difficult place	**A blog post** ■ A blog about a busy place ■ *and, also,* and *too*	■ Talk about the lives of people in a picture ■ Talk about good and bad times to call someone ■ Tell a friend what you are doing right now ■ Talk about your news **Time to speak** ■ Talk about your life these days
■ Ask for and give for opinions **Real-world strategy** ■ Explain and say more about an idea	**Technology Talks** ■ A podcast about computers		**A comment** ■ Comments about an online post ■ Quotations	■ Discuss activities you do ■ Talk about skills you have ■ Talk about what you can and can't do at work ■ Ask and answer questions in a job interview **Time to speak** ■ Discuss national skills
■ Ask for and give information **Real-world strategy** ■ Ask someone to repeat something		**Places to go near Puno** ■ A travel guide	**A description** ■ A description of a place ■ Imperatives to give advice	■ Talk about a place you like ■ Describe people and places in a picture ■ Talk about organizing a trip ■ Ask for information at an airport store **Time to speak** ■ Talk about planning a vacation
■ Make, accept, and refuse suggestions **Real-world strategy** ■ Say why you can't do something	**Montevideo** ■ A TV travel show		**An invitation** ■ An event invitation ■ Contractions	■ Talk about your plans for the future ■ Talk about outdoor activities in your city ■ Talk about clothes to take for a trip ■ Talk about where to go out for dinner **Time to speak** ■ Plan a fun weekend in your home city
■ Express uncertainty **Real-world strategy** ■ Take time to think		**Picturing memories** ■ An article about things people keep	**An email** ■ An email to a friend ■ Paragraphs and topic sentences	■ Describe a happy time in your life ■ Talk about things you remember ■ Talk about colors you remember from when you were a child ■ Talk about people in a movie **Time to speak** ■ Present your memories of a TV show from your past
■ Offer, request and accept food and drink **Real-world strategy** ■ Use *so* and *really* to make words stronger	**Where do you want to eat?** ■ A conversation about restaurants on a food app		**A review** ■ A restaurant review ■ Commas in lists	■ Describe a good meal you had ■ Talk about snacks and small meals you like ■ Talk about a meal you had in a restaurant ■ Ask for food in a restaurant or at a friend's house **Time to speak** ■ Design a menu for a new restaurant

CLASSROOM LANGUAGE

🔊 **1.02** **Get started**

Hi. / Hello.

What's your name?

My name is _____.

This is my class.

This is my partner.

This is my teacher.

Ask for help

I don't understand.

I have a question.

How do you say _____ in English?

What does _____ mean?

How do you spell _____?

Can you repeat that, please?

Sorry, what page?

Your teacher

I'm your teacher.

Open your book.

Close your book.

Go to page _____.

Do you have any questions?

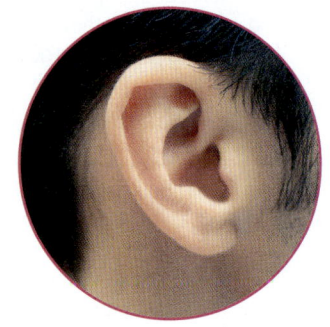
Listen.

Say.

Read.

Write.

Watch.

Work in pairs.

Work in groups.

START SPEAKING

A   Say what you see in the picture. Who are the people? Are they at work or do they have free time? Where are they?

B   Are they busy now? Do they have a busy life?

C   Talk about things:

■ they do *and* you do.

■ you do, but they don't.

■ they do, but you don't.

A GOOD TIME TO CALL

1 LANGUAGE IN CONTEXT

A 🔊 **2.02** David calls his sister Ariana on the phone. Read and listen. (Circle) the correct answers.

1 Ariana is *the mother / the daughter*.

2 Jason is *Ariana's son / Ariana's husband*.

3 Stevie is *Ariana's son / Ariana's daughter*.

4 Julia is *Ariana's sister / Stevie's sister*.

🔊 **2.02 Audio script**

David	Hi, Ariana. It's David. Are you busy? Is this a good time to call?
Ariana	Um, well, I'm **cooking** breakfast right now, and Jason's **helping** the children— Jason, Stevie isn't drinking his milk.
David	Oh, yeah. It's a school day today.
Ariana	That's right, so …
David	What time do they leave for school?
Ariana	Usually at 8:00, but we're running late today — Jason, give this to the kids, OK? Thanks. — OK, David, they're eating breakfast now.
David	Do they like their classes?
Ariana	Yes, and they're learning a lot — Julia, you're not eating. Please eat your breakfast now! — Sorry, David. This isn't a good time to talk.

B 🔊 **2.02** Read and listen again. Is David busy now? Why does Ariana say *"This isn't a good time to talk."*?

GLOSSARY
kids (*n*) children (informal)
running late (*phrase*) you are late

2 VOCABULARY: Activities around the house

A 🔊 **2.03** Look at the pictures. Listen and repeat.

1 I'm cleaning the kitchen.

2 I'm cooking dinner.

3 I'm washing my hair.

4 I'm brushing my teeth.

5 I'm doing the dishes.

6 I'm helping my daughters. They're taking a bath.

B Add the words in the box to the verbs.

breakfast	the dog	my hair	my homework	~~my room~~	a shower

1 **clean** the kitchen / _my room_

2 **cook** dinner / _____

3 **wash** my hair / _____

4 **brush** my teeth / _____

5 **take** a bath / _____

6 **do** the dishes / _____

C ▶ Now do the vocabulary exercises for 7.1 on page 146.

D PAIR WORK Do you do your homework <u>and</u> talk on the phone? What other activities do you do at the same time? For ideas, watch June's video.

REAL STUDENT

Do you do the things June does?

3 GRAMMAR: Present continuous statements

A **Circle** the correct answer. Use the sentences in the grammar box to help you.

1 Use the present continuous to talk about **things happening right now or around now / finished things**.
2 Sentences 1, 2, and 3 in the grammar box are about **right now / around now**.
3 Sentence 4 is about **right now / around now**.
4 To make the present continuous, use *am/is/are* and a **verb + -ing / verb + -s**.

> ### Present continuous statements
>
> 1 I'm **cooking** breakfast right now.
> 2 Jason, Stevie **isn't drinking** his milk.
>
> 3 Julia, you**'re not eating** your breakfast.
> 4 They**'re learning** a lot at school this year.

B Complete the sentences in the present continuous. Use an affirmative or negative form of the verbs in parentheses ( ).

1 He _____ (take) a bath. He's in the shower.
2 I _____ (do) my homework now. It's really difficult.
3 Carola isn't studying right now. She _____ (watch) TV.
4 My parents _____ (wash) the car. They're having lunch now.
5 I _____ (brush) my hair. I'm brushing my teeth.
6 You _____ (help) your friends with their English. You're really nice!
7 My cat loves milk. It _____ (drink) milk right now.

C Now go to page 135. Look at the grammar chart and do the grammar exercise for 7.1.

D Think about four of your friends. What are they doing or not doing now? Write sentences about each person. Then check your accuracy.

Teresa isn't studying. She's playing games on her phone.

✓ **ACCURACY** CHECK

Use the present continuous for things you're doing now. Use the simple present for things you do regularly.

Just a minute. ~~I talk~~ on the phone. ✗
Just a minute. I'm talking on the phone. ✓
I talk on the phone every day. ✓
I'm talking on the phone every day. ✗

4 SPEAKING

A **Think of what you're usually doing at the times of day below. Is it a good or bad time to call you?**

- Monday, 7:30 a.m.
- Tuesday, 10:00 a.m.
- Wednesday, 1:30 p.m
- Thursday, 3:30 p.m.
- Friday, 9:30 p.m
- Saturday, 11:00 a.m.
- Sunday, 6:00 p.m.

B **PAIR WORK** Take turns choosing times in exercise 4A. For each time, "call" your partner and ask, *"Is this a good time to call?"* Listen to the answers. Is your partner a busy person?

Hi, is this a good time to call?

No, sorry. I'm having dinner with my family.

1 VOCABULARY: Transportation

A 🔊 2.04 **Look at the pictures. Listen and repeat.**

take the bus/ train/subway

go to a store / your parents' house

walk

be at the bus stop / train station

carry a bag

wait

ride your/my bike

be on the bus/train/subway

drive

B Circle the correct words to complete the sentences.

1 I *ride my bike / am at the bus stop* to class every day.

2 I'm *waiting / walking* for a friend right now.

3 We *are on the train / take the subway* to work on Fridays.

4 Are you *carrying / walking* right now?

5 I'm *at the train station / to the mall* right now.

C ▶ **Now do the vocabulary exercises for 7.2 on page 146.**

D GROUP WORK **How do you usually get to the places in the box? For ideas, watch Julieth's video.**

English class   the supermarket   work/college   your best friend's house

REAL STUDENT *Do you use the same transportation as Julieth?*

2 LANGUAGE IN CONTEXT

A **Read the text messages. Where is Inna going? Why?**

B **Read the text messages again. Correct the sentences.**

1 Inna is sending text messages to ~~her father~~.   *Rob*

2 Inna is taking the bus to the mall.   _____

3 Inna's dad is waiting at his house.   _____

4 Inna is carrying a big bag.   _____

5 Today is Inna's dad's birthday.   _____

> **INSIDER ENGLISH**
>
> People often write *ha ha* (the sound of a laugh) in informal writing. It means they think something is funny.

12:00 PM

Hey, Inna. Are you going to work?

No, I'm not. **I'm on the bus**. I'm **going to my parents' house**.

You usually **ride your bike** there. Why are you **taking the bus**?

Because I'm **carrying** a big plant. Oh, **I'm at the bus stop** now, and my dad's **waiting**.

😂 Ha ha! A plant! Why are you carrying a plant?

Because plants don't **walk**! 😄😄😄 Really it's for my mom's birthday.

Oh, wow! Say happy birthday from me.

3 GRAMMAR: present continuous questions

A (Circle) the correct answer. Use the questions in the grammar box to help you.

1 Use *are* and *is* **at the beginning / in the middle** of *yes/no* questions.

2 Use *are* and *is* **before / after** question words (for example, *What* or *When*) in information questions.

> ### Present continuous questions
>
> | *Yes/no* questions | Information questions |
> |---|---|
> | **Are** you **going** to work? | **Why is** he **carrying** a plant? |
> | **Is** she **carrying** a plant? | **Who are** they **waiting** for? |
> | **Are** they **waiting** at the bus stop? | **What are** you **doing**? |

B Complete the questions with the present continuous form of the verbs in the box. Then match the questions and the answers below.

> carry   do   go   listen   ride

1 _____ Josh _____ his bike in the park right now?

2 What _____ Kim and Todd _____?

3 _____ the children _____ to music right now?

4 Why _____ Jamal _____ a big bag?

5 Where _____ Lydia _____ now?

____ **a** Because he's taking a lot of books to class.

____ **b** Yes, they are.

____ **c** She's walking to her friend's house.

____ **d** No, he isn't. He's running by the lake.

____ **e** They're driving to the beach.

C ▶ Now go to page 135. Look at the grammar charts and do the grammar exercise for 7.2.

D PAIR WORK Imagine what people in your family are doing right now. Ask and answer questions.

> What's your sister doing right now?

4 SPEAKING

FIND IT

A Imagine you're going somewhere and carrying something interesting or funny. Use the ideas below or your own ideas. Then decide where you are going and your transportation.

> a big bag   a small chair   an expensive picture

B PAIR WORK What is your partner doing? Ask and answer questions.

> Hi, Anna. What are you doing?

> I'm carrying 100 cookies. I'm at the subway station.

7.3   A NEW LIFE

1   FUNCTIONAL LANGUAGE

A   Look at the people. Are they having a long or a short conversation? How long are your phone calls?

B   ◀)) 2.05 Luana is calling her friend Jennifer. Read and listen. What's new in Luana's life?

◀)) 2.05 Audio script

Jennifer	**Hello.**
Luana	**Hi**, Jennifer. **It's** Luana.
Jennifer	**Hey**, Luana!
Luana	**How's it going?**
Jennifer	**Not bad, thanks. How are you doing?**
Luana	**Good, thanks.** Well, I'm busy.
Jennifer	Really? What are you doing these days?
Luana	I have a new job, in Monterrey.
Jennifer	Oh, wow! *Monterrey*? So you're not living in Mexico City now.
Luana	That's right. I'm living in Monterrey. I live in a new building. It's expensive, but it's very nice. And I have a new boyfriend.
Jennifer	Really? Great! You have a new *life*! I want to hear all about it!

C   Complete the chart with expressions in **bold** from the conversation above.

Answering the phone and greeting people	Asking people how they are	Responding
1 ____Hello____ .	How's it ⁵ _____ ? (*How's = How is*)	Not ⁸ _____ , thanks.
2 _____ , Jennifer.	How ⁶ _____ you	⁹ _____ , thanks.
3 _____ Luana.	⁷ _____ ?	I'm fine.
4 _____ , Luana!	How are you?	

D   ◀)) 2.06 [PAIR WORK] Put the phone conversation in the correct order. Listen and check. Then practice with a partner.

____ Good, thanks. How's it going?

_3_ Hey, Andrew! How are you doing?

_1_ Hello.

____ Not bad.

____ Hi, Francisco. It's Andrew.

2 REAL-WORLD STRATEGY

REACTING TO NEWS

People often say *oh* after they hear good news, ordinary news, and bad news.

Good news 😄
Oh, wow!

Ordinary news 😐
Oh.

Bad news 🙁
Oh, no!

Luana *I have a new job.*
Luana *I'm busy.*
Luana *My apartment is very expensive.*

Jennifer *Oh, wow!*
Jennifer *Oh.*
Jennifer *Oh, no!*

A **Read the information in the box about reacting to news. Then look at the examples. What does Jennifer think is: good news, ordinary news, and bad news?**

B 🔊 **2.07** **Listen to a conversation. What news does the man give?**

Ordinary news: *He's in his car.*   Good news: _____

Bad news: _____

C 🔊 **2.07** **Listen again. How does the woman react to the different types of news?**

D ▶ PAIR WORK **Student A: Go to page 158. Student B: Go to page 160. Follow the instructions.**

3 PRONUNCIATION: Saying *-ing* at the end of the word

A 🔊 **2.08** **Listen. Complete the words.**

1 How are you do_____ ?   2 I'm liv_____ in Dallas.   3 Where are you go_____ ?

B 🔊 **2.09** **Listen. Focus on the *-in* and *-ing* sounds. (Circle) the phrase you hear.**

1 a learn in Spanish   b learning Spanish   4 a study in nature   b studying nature
2 a call in the restaurant b calling the restaurant 5 a carry in a bag   b carrying a bag
3 a help in my school   b helping my school   6 a shop in malls   b shopping malls

C 🔊 **2.10** PAIR WORK **Listen to the conversations. Then practice with a partner. Listen for the *-ing* sound.**

1 A How are you do**ing**?
   B Not bad. I'm work**ing** in Monterrey now.
2 A Are you liv**ing** in Mexico City now?
   B No, I'm liv**ing** in Monterrey.

3 A Where are you go**ing**?
   B We're go**ing** to the Italian restaurant over there.

4 SPEAKING

PAIR WORK **Imagine you're calling your partner. Start the call, and then talk about some news. Use some of the questions below. React to the things your partner says. Then change roles.**

How are you doing?   Are you busy?
What are you doing right now?   What about you?

Hey, Ali. It's Clara.   Hey, Clara! How are you doing?

CHAOS!

1 READING

A SKIM Skim the text. Where is the man? What is on his laptop?

JAMIE'S BLOG

HOME   ABOUT   BLOG

**Bloggers sometimes write from difficult places: mountains, deserts, rainforests …
So today, my blog is from a difficult place, too. I'm writing from my living room.**

Why is it difficult to write in here? Well, my brother's playing soccer (yes, in the living room.) The ball is going *BOOM-BOOM-BOOM* on the wall near my table and chair. My sister's doing her homework. Every two minutes, she asks me a question: "What's 15% of 500? What's 50% of 320?" So, really, *I'm* doing her homework.

The TV is on, but I don't know why. My mom's talking about work on the phone, so she isn't watching TV. And my dad isn't watching it. He's in the kitchen: *PSSSSSS, CRASH, BANG!* He's cooking – I think. And the cat doesn't like TV. But she likes laptops. She's walking on my laptop … and now she's going to sleep! How do I work in this place? It's chaos!

B READ FOR DETAILS Read the blog again. Find words to complete the chart.

5 people in the family	me
3 technology words	
2 pieces of furniture	
2 rooms	
1 animal	

C PAIR WORK   THINK CRITICALLY Which people from exercise 1B are busy? having fun?

2 WRITING

A Jodi is a college student. She's helping at a school for a week. Read her blog. What <u>six</u> things are the children doing? What <u>three</u> things is Jodi doing? What <u>one</u> thing are the children <u>and</u> Jodi doing?

Jodi's Blog

Home   About   Blog

Busy!

April 11

I'm helping a teacher at a school this week. Today, I'm writing my blog on a school bus. We're going to the beach. There are 25 kids on the bus, and they're nine and ten years old. Wow, they're making a lot of noise! They're busy, too. Some kids are talking. Some kids are playing music on their phones. Some are singing. Three boys are playing games on a tablet. Also, the children are eating cookies.
What about me? Well, I'm cleaning their hands
and washing their faces.
And I'm answering millions of questions
from the kids. They're happy.
The teacher is happy, too.
But this is difficult for me.
Am I getting old?

GLOSSARY
noise (*n*) a sound or sounds, usually loud
millions (*quantifier*) a lot (informal)

B **WRITING SKILLS** People use *also* and *too* to add information. <u>Underline</u> the words *also* and *too* in the blog. Then (circle) the correct words in the rules, below.

Use *too* at the **beginning** / **end** of a sentence.

Use a comma (,) **before** / **after** you write *too*.

Use *also* at the **beginning** / **end** of a sentence.

Use a *comma* (,) **before** / **after** you write *also*.

WRITE IT

C Imagine you're in a very busy place: at home, at college, at work, on a bus, or at a party. Write a blog about the activities happening around you. Use the title "Busy!"

D **PAIR WORK** Compare your blog with a partner. How many activities does your partner describe?

REGISTER CHECK

People sometimes use *And*, *Also*, or *But* at the beginning of sentences in speaking and informal writing. In formal writing, people usually don't begin sentences with these words.

And I'm answering millions of questions from the kids.

Also, the children are eating cookies.

But this is difficult for me.

7.5 TIME TO SPEAK
Your life these days

A **PREPARE** Read the note and questions below. Which topic is interesting for you? Which topic is boring?

> You are with a group of people. They are your friends, but you hardly ever see them. What do you say? Here are some ideas!

Topics	Main question	Follow-up questions
Work and school	Are you going to college?	Are your classes easy or difficult? Are you doing a lot of homework these days?
	What classes are you taking?	Do you like your classes? Why or why not?
	Where are you working these days?	Are you working every day? Is your job interesting? Is it difficult?
Free time	What are you reading these days?	Is it good? Who's the writer?
	What are you watching on TV?	Is it interesting? Is it funny? Who's in it?
	What music are you listening to?	Who's your favorite singer? What's your favorite band?
	Do you play video games?	Which games are you playing right now?
	Are you going out a lot these days?	Where do you go? What's your favorite place?
	Are you playing sports?	What sports do you play? Where?
Home life	How is your family?	Are you living with them now?
	Are you living in a new place?	Is it an apartment or house? Do you like it? Is it close to work/school?
	Are you cooking a lot these days?	Do you cook for other people?

B **ROLE PLAY** Imagine you are at a party. Talk to different people about different topics. Ask and answer some of the questions from the chart.

C **AGREE** Talk about popular things from your conversations. What are a lot of people doing these days?

➤➤ *To check your progress, go to page 154.* ➤➤

USEFUL PHRASES

 PREPARE
I like / don't like …
I think … is interesting/boring.
And you?

 ROLE PLAY
Hi, [name]. How's it going?
Hey, [name]! What are you doing these days?

 AGREE
(Work and school / free time / home life) is a popular topic.
A lot of people are doing …

- talk about your skills and abilities
- say what you can and can't do at work or school
- say why you're the right person for a job
- write an online comment with your opinion
- talk about what people in your country are good at

YOU'RE GOOD!

8

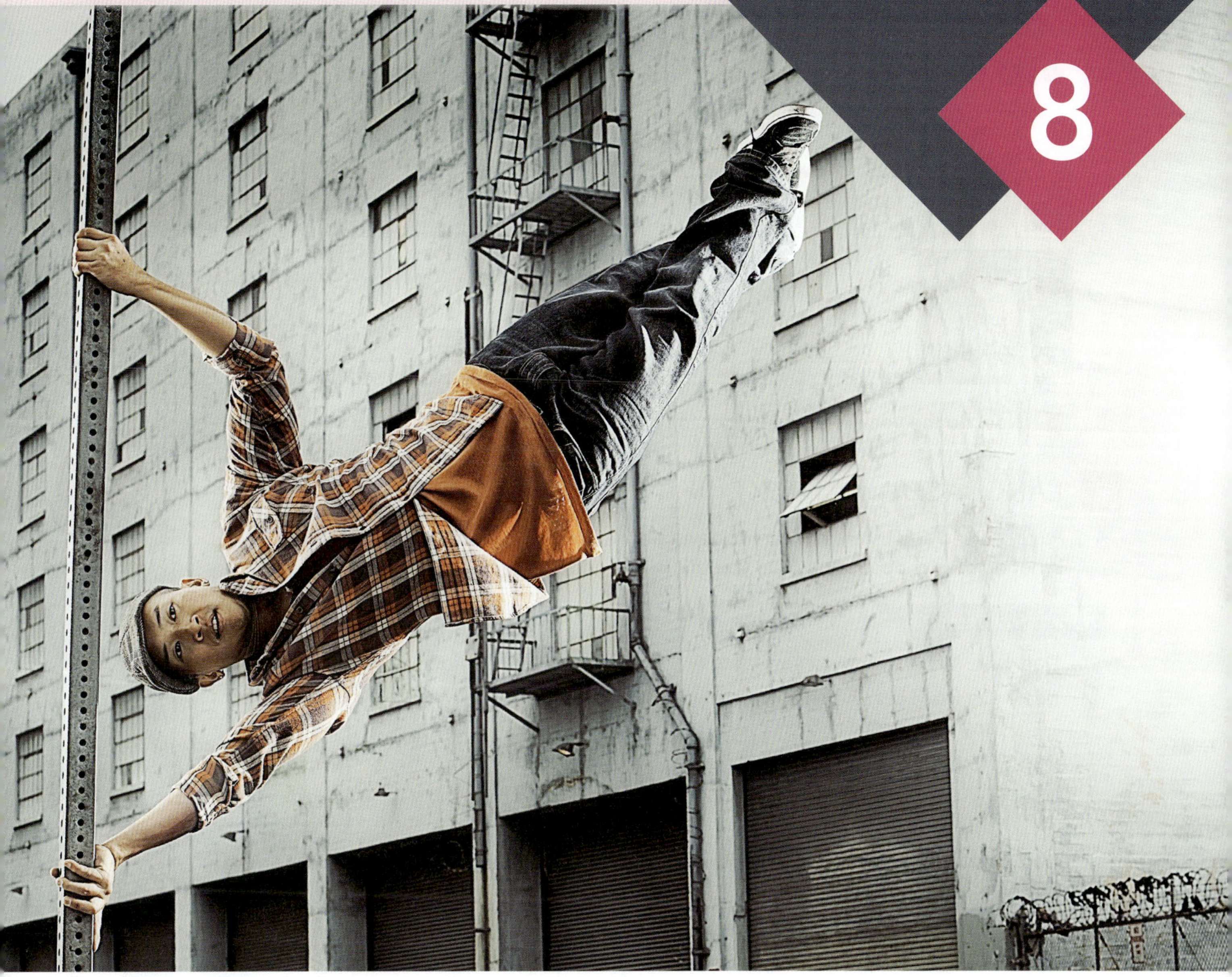

START SPEAKING

A   Look at the picture. Where is this person? What is he doing?

B   Do you think this is a difficult activity? Do you think it's fun?

C   Talk to a partner about fun or difficult activities you do. For ideas, watch Anderson's video.

REAL STUDENT

What does Anderson do? Do you think it's fun, difficult, or both?

SHE LIKES MUSIC, BUT SHE CAN'T DANCE!

LESSON OBJECTIVE
- talk about your skills and abilities

1 VOCABULARY: Verbs to describe skills

A 🔊 **2.11** Listen and repeat the skills in the pictures. Which are fun skills? Which are difficult skills?

 dance

 draw

 fix things

 read music

 paint

 play the guitar

 sing

 skateboard

 snowboard

 speak two languages

 surf

 swim

B ▶ **Now do the vocabulary exercises for 8.1 on page 147.**

2 LANGUAGE IN CONTEXT

A 🔊 **2.12** Read and listen. Who are Mia and her dad talking about? What do they choose to buy? Do you think it's a good idea?

🔊 **2.12 Audio script**

Dad	So, Mia. You know it's your mom's birthday next month, right?
Mia	Oh wow! Let's buy her something really cool. Do you have any ideas?
Dad	Hmm. How about some art classes? She can **draw**.
Mia	Or what about singing lessons? She likes music and can **play the guitar**.
Dad	I don't think that's a good idea. She thinks she can't **sing**, and she's very shy about it.
Mia	Hmm. What about dance lessons? Can she **dance** well?
Dad	No, she can't. She's terrible at it. It's really funny – she can **read music**, but she can't dance!
Mia	*You* can't dance, Dad. I know! Let's buy you both some dance lessons!
Dad	Great idea! Wait a minute – what?

INSIDER ENGLISH

You can use *So* to start talking about a topic.

So, Mia. You know it's your mom's birthday next month, right?

GLOSSARY
terrible (*adj*) very bad

B 🔊 **2.12** Read and listen again. What can Mia's mom do? What can't she do? Complete the sentences.

1 Mia's mom can _____, _____, and _____.

2 She can't _____ and _____.

C **PAIR WORK** Talk to a partner. Which things in exercise 1A do you often do? Which things do you never do? For ideas, watch Larissa's video.

 **REAL STUDENT**

Do you often do the same things as Larissa?

3 GRAMMAR: *can* and *can't* for ability; *well*

A (Circle) the correct answers. Use the sentences in the grammar box and the information in the Notice box to help you.

1 Use *can* / *can't* to talk about things you don't do well or don't know how to do.

2 Use *can* / *can't* to talk about things you do well or know how to do.

3 With *he, she,* and *it*, **do** / **do not** add *-s* to the verb after *can* or *can't*.

can and *can't* (= *can not*) for ability		
I **can** swim.	I **can't** play the guitar.	**Can** you fix things?
She **can** draw.	He **can't** sing well.	**Can** he surf?
We **can** surf well.	They **can't** read music.	**Can** they speak two languages?

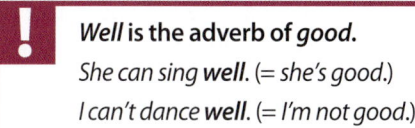

! *Well* is the adverb of *good*.
She can sing well. (= she's good.)
I can't dance well. (= I'm not good.)

B (Circle) the correct answers to complete the sentences.

1 I swim every day. I *can* / *can't* swim well.

2 Sorry. My dad *can* / *can't* fix your car. He's not a mechanic.

3 You can draw really well, Tomas. What other things *can* / *can't* you do?

4 She *can* / *can't* drive, and she doesn't have a car.

5 You *can* / *can't* skateboard really well! Can you teach me?

6 **A** Can you play the guitar, Robbie?

 B No, I *can* / *can't*.

C ▶ Now go to page 136. Look at the grammar chart and do the grammar exercise for 8.1.

D Write <u>five</u> questions to ask people in your class about their skills. Use vocabulary from exercise 1A. Then check your accuracy.

1 Can you _____ ?

2 Can you _____ ?

3 Can you _____ ?

4 Can you _____ ?

5 Can you _____ ?

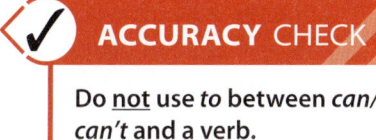

✓ **ACCURACY** CHECK

Do <u>not</u> use *to* between *can/can't* and a verb.

Can you ~~to~~ fix bikes? ✗
Can you fix bikes? ✓

4 SPEAKING

A | GROUP WORK | **Ask and answer your questions from exercise 3D. Say how well you do the skills.**

Can you play the guitar?

No, I can't. What about you?

Yes, I can. I can play it really well.

B | GROUP WORK | **What skill can everyone in your group do? Who can do it really well?**

8.2 HAPPY WORKERS = GREAT WORKERS?

LESSON OBJECTIVE
■ say what you can and can't do at work or school

1 LANGUAGE IN CONTEXT

A Look at the offices in the pictures on pages 78 and 79. How are they different from other offices? Do you like them? Are they good places to work?

B Read the article. What activities can you do in a happy office?

Not just an office … an ☺FFICE

Who can you find in all great **companies**? Great **workers**. And what's true for all great workers? They're happy because happy people do a great job.

How can companies make their workers happy? They can pay them a lot of money, of course, but money can't make people happy – not always. A great company can also give its workers a happy **office**. Happy offices aren't just ordinary offices with desks, phones, and computers – and they're not *just* for work.

What can you do in a happy office? The short answer is, you can **work hard** *and* have fun. You can run or play basketball with **your coworkers** and **have a meeting** at the same time. This is a great way to **think** of new ideas. You can work in a cool room with big chairs and no table or **take a break** in a room with a lot of plants (like a forest!) In some offices, you can come to work with your dog!

GLOSSARY
all (*det*) 100% of something
pay (*v*) give someone money for their work
ordinary (*adj*) usual, normal

2 VOCABULARY: Work

A 🔊 **2.13** Find the words below in the article. Then listen and repeat.

| company | workers | office | work hard | have a meeting | think | take a break | your coworkers |

B Match the words from exercise 2A with the definitions.

1 a workplace, with desks and chairs
2 the people you work with
3 a business – for example, Microsoft or Toyota
4 the people in a company
5 do a lot of work
6 stop work for a short time – for example, to have coffee
7 have ideas, or find answers to problems
8 get together with people at work and talk about business

C ▶ Now do the vocabulary exercises for 8.2 on page 148.

FIND IT

D GROUP WORK What other activities can you do in a happy office? Which companies have happy workers? You can go online to find examples.

3 GRAMMAR: *can* and *can't* for possibility

A (Circle) the correct answers. Use the sentences in the grammar box to help you.

1 Use *can* to talk about things that are **possible** / **not possible**.

2 Question words (*Who, What, Where, Why,* and *How*) go **before** / **after** *can* or *can't* to ask about possibility.

can and can't for possibility

You **can** work hard and have fun.

She **can** take a break any time.

Your dog **can't** come to work with you.

What **can't** they do in the office?

How **can** companies make their workers happy?

Where **can** you have a meeting?

B Put the words in the correct order to make questions. Then match them to the answers (a–e) below.

1 we / have / lunch? / can / Where _____

2 the / restaurant? / How / get / to / can / I _____

3 can / What / eat? / we _____

4 have / the / meeting? / we / can / When _____

5 I / this / message? / send / can / How _____

_____ a We can have some cookies.

_____ b You can email it from your phone.

_____ c Tuesday is good for me.

_____ d In the company restaurant.

_____ e Go straight, and then turn left.

C ▶ Now go to page 137. Look at the grammar chart and do the grammar exercise for 8.2.

D Write questions about a company or school to ask if it's a good place to work or study.

1 What can _____ ?

2 Where can _____ ?

3 How can _____ ?

4 SPEAKING

PAIR WORK Talk to a partner about things you can and can't do at your company or school. Ask your questions from exercise 3D.

What can you do at lunchtime?

You can go to …

ARE YOU THE RIGHT PERSON?

1 FUNCTIONAL LANGUAGE

A Look at the picture. Where are the people? What are they doing?

B 🔊 **2.14** Read and listen. What <u>three</u> things can the man do well?

🔊 **2.14 Audio script**

A Can we speak in English for five minutes?

B Yes, we can.

A Great. So, are you the right person for this job?

B Yes. **I think so.**

A Why? In a very short answer, please.

B Because I can work well with people on a team. **I think that** teamwork is very important.

A I see. **Why do you think** it's important?

B Because a company is a big team. I mean, it's a group of people, and you work with them every day.

A And why are *you* good on a team?

B Because I like people, and I can communicate well.

A That's great. **I think that** good communication is important. But **I don't think** it's the only important thing. What other things can you do well?

B I can speak two languages. I mean, I speak Spanish and English.

C Complete the chart with expressions in **bold** from the conversation above.

Asking for opinions	Giving opinions
What do you think ? ¹ _____ do you think (that) … ?	I think ² _____ . I don't think so. I ³ _____ (that) … I ⁴ _____ think (that) …

D 🔊 **2.15** [PAIR WORK] Complete the conversations with words from exercise 1C. Listen and check. Then ask and answer the questions with a partner. Answer with your ideas.

1 A I think video games are great. What do you think?

   B I _____ they're very cool. They're boring.

2 A _____ do you _____ cell phones are important?

   B They're useful. We communicate with our phones.

3 A Do you think soccer is a good sport?

   B No. I _____ . I like basketball.

4 A Are you good at music?

   B I _____ . I sing and play the guitar really well.

2 REAL-WORLD STRATEGY

EXPLAINING AND SAYING MORE ABOUT AN IDEA

Use *I mean* to explain or say more about an idea.

A company is a big team. I mean, it's a group of people, and you work with them every day.

I can speak two languages. I mean, I speak Spanish and English.

A   Read about explaining and saying more about an idea in the box above. Look at what the man says. What idea does he explain? What idea does he give more information about?

B   🔊 **2.16** Listen to a conversation. What does Lori want to do? When does she have free time?

C   🔊 **2.16** Listen to the conversation again. Complete the chart with the sentences you hear.

Idea	Explanation/more information
I work really hard.	I mean, I ¹_____ about ²_____ a day.
I'm not busy.	I mean, I ³_____ in a restaurant ⁴_____ _____, but I have free time in the ⁵_____.

D   ▶ PAIR WORK **Student A: Go to page 158. Student B: Go to page 160. Follow the instructions.**

3 PRONUNCIATION: Saying groups of words

A   🔊 **2.17** Listen for the space (= short pause) between the words (/). Which sentences do you hear, A or B?

1 **A** Can we speak in English / for five minutes?
   B Can we speak in / English for five minutes?

2 **A** What other things can / you do well?
   B What other things / can you do well?

B   🔊 **2.18** Listen to the sentences. Write a pause mark (/) in each sentence.

1 I'm good on a team because I can communicate well.

2 I can speak two languages and I can play the guitar.

3 I work in a restaurant at night but I'm free in the mornings.

4 I think that good communication is important but I don't think it's the only important thing.

C   PAIR WORK **Practice the sentences in exercise 3B with a partner. Take turns. Can your partner hear the spaces between the words?**

4 SPEAKING

A   **Choose a job from the box or your own idea. Think about why you are the right person for the job.**

an art teacher	a chef at a restaurant	a hotel clerk
a singer in a band	a soccer player	

B   PAIR WORK **Tell a partner your job from exercise 4A. Your partner interviews you for the job. Then change roles.**

Are you the right person for this job?   *I think so. I …*

COMPUTERS AND OUR JOBS

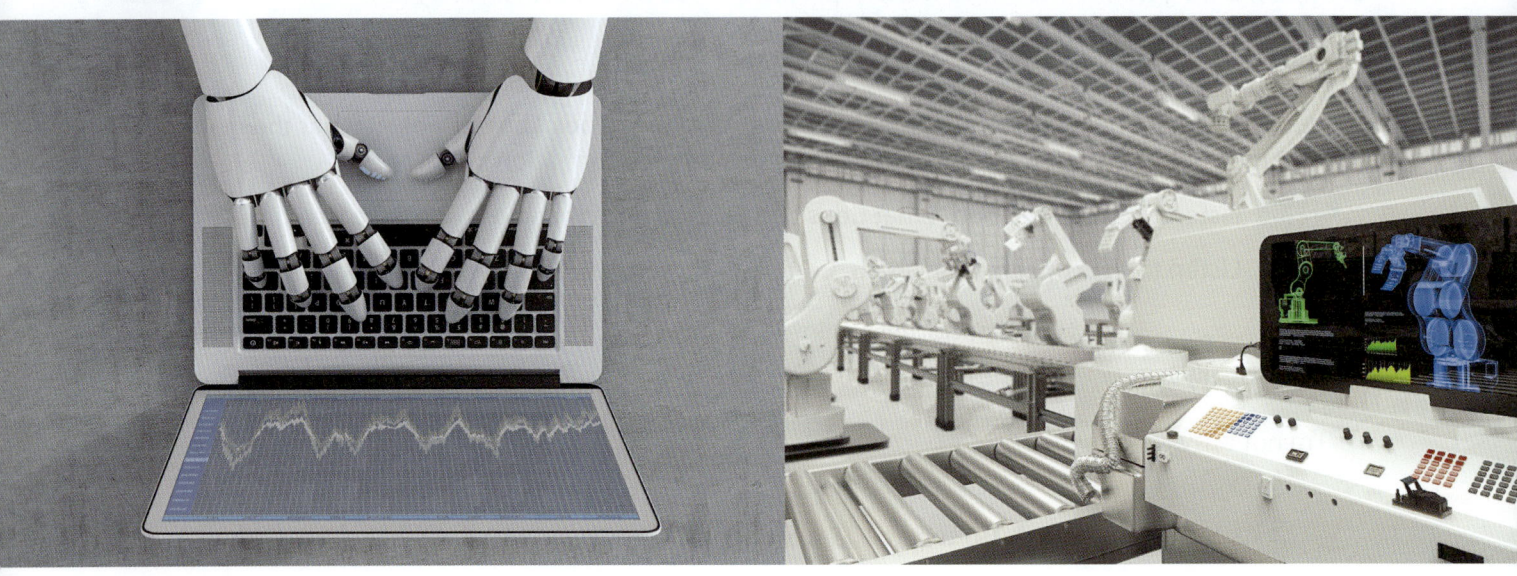

1 LISTENING

A Chris is the host of the podcast *Technology Talks*. Look at the pictures above. What is today's podcast about?

B 🔊 **2.19** **LISTEN FOR DETAILS** Listen to the podcast. Who is Joanna Ramos? What does she say computers <u>can't</u> do?

C 🔊 **2.19** **LISTEN FOR SUPPORTING DETAILS** Listen again. Check (✓) the supporting details Joanna gives.

Jobs for computers	New jobs for people
☐ make cars	☐ make computers
☐ drive cars	☐ start computer companies
☐ call people on the phone	☐ make cars
☐ talk	☐ be a computer's voice
☐ think	☐ make phones

D **PAIR WORK** **THINK CRITICALLY** Who thinks computers are a good thing: Joanna or Chris?

2 PRONUNCIATION: Listening for *can* and *can't*

A 🔊 **2.20** Listen. Write the missing words.

1 What _____ computers do?

2 They _____ make cars.

3 A computer _____ make 100% of a car.

B 🔊 **2.21** Listen. Do you hear *can* or *can't*? (Circle) the correct words.

1 can / can't   2 can / can't

3 can / can't   4 can / can't

3 WRITING

A Read three people's online comments about the podcast. Which person thinks Joanna is correct? Which person <u>doesn't</u> think Joanna is correct? What's your favorite comment?

TECHNOLOGY TALKS:
Interview with Joanna Ramos

JUNE 1, 11:30 A.M.

Kaito, Tokyo

I don't think Joanna Ramos is right. Computers *are* a problem. Robots are taking all our jobs! They can say hello to people in stores and hotels, they can cook, they can play music, they can clean buildings, they can make cars … What jobs CAN'T they do? Joanna says, "People make computers." Well, I think robots can make computers now. They're *very* smart.

Ruby, Miami

Computers and robots can do a lot of things, but they don't have feelings: they're not happy, and they're not sad. Feelings are important for many jobs. For example, teachers, doctors, and nurses work with people, so feelings are important. I don't like the idea of robot doctors!

Arturo, Mexico City

Computers are cheap. I mean, companies pay people for their work, but they don't pay their robots or computers. And computers work hard. But I think Ruby is right. Computers don't have feelings. Joanna is right, too. She says, "They are taking *some* of our jobs." Not *all* of them. She also says, "There are a lot of new jobs, too." That's true. It's not a problem.

GLOSSARY
robot (*n*) a machine with a computer in it

B **WRITING SKILLS** Sometimes we want to write another person's words. Their words are quotations. Read the rules below. Then ⊙circle⊙ all the capital letters and punctuation marks in sentences 1–3.

- Use quotation marks (" ") around other people's words.
- Put a comma (,) after *says*.
- Start the quotation with a capital letter (A, B, C, …).

1 Joanna says, "People make computers."
2 She says, "They are taking *some* of our jobs."
3 She also says, "There are a lot of new jobs, too."

REGISTER CHECK

In informal writing and speaking, people often use *says* to quote (= give) another person's words.

In an online comment: *Joanna says, "People make computers."*

In formal writing, people often use *said*.

In a newspaper article: *Joanna Ramos said, "A computer can't make 100% of a car."*

 **WRITE IT**

C Read the ideas from Joanna's interview in exercise 1C. Then write an online comment. Give your opinion about computers and jobs. Quote some of Joanna's words.

D **GROUP WORK** Read your group's comments. Do you have the same or different ideas?

TIME TO SPEAK
National skills

A **PREPARE** Match the skills in the box to the pictures. Which three skills are <u>not</u> in the pictures?

cook   dance   make movies   paint   play soccer   sing   snowboard   surf

B **DISCUSS** Where can people do the things from exercise A really well? For each skill, say the name of a city, region/area, or country. Then compare your ideas with your group.

C **DECIDE** Read the information in the box on the right. Talk to a partner about the question in the box. Together, think of <u>three</u> skills for the video.

D **AGREE** Compare everyone's ideas. Choose your class' <u>three</u> favorite ideas for the video.

>> *To check your progress, go to page 154.* >>

CAN YOU HELP US?

We want to make a YouTube™ video about our country and why it's great. The title is "We're good!" The video is about the skills people have here. What can we do *really* well in this country? Please send us your ideas!

USEFUL PHRASES

DISCUSS
Where can people cook really well?
Chinese food is always great.
I think people can cook really well in Rome and Naples.
What do you think?

DECIDE
What can we do really well in this country?
We can do … well.
I agree. / I disagree.
Our three skills for the video are …

AGREE
What are your ideas?
Good idea!
Our three favorite skills are …

UNIT OBJECTIVES

- talk about travel and vacations
- make travel plans
- ask for information in a store
- write a description of a place
- plan a vacation for someone

START SPEAKING

A Look at the picture. Where is the woman? Is it difficult to get to this place?

B What do you do in your free time? Do you go to new places?

C Think of a place you like. Talk about it. Say why it's good. For ideas, watch Julieth's video.

REAL STUDENT

What's Julieth's place? Do you agree it's a good place to go?

I LOVE IT HERE!

LESSON OBJECTIVE
■ talk about travel and vacations

1 LANGUAGE IN CONTEXT

A **Kaitlin and her friends are on vacation. Read Kaitlin's posts. Where do they go?**

B **Read again. Check (✓) the sentences that are true. Correct the false ones.**

☐ 1 Kaitlin takes a bus to San Diego.

☐ 2 They go to their hotel on Thursday.

☐ 3 They are in San Diego on Friday.

☐ 4 They go to a zoo on Saturday.

☐ 5 Kaitlin and her friends have a bad vacation.

FROM MY SMALL TOWN TO A BIG CITY

● PROFILE
▶ LOG OUT

THURSDAY MORNING

Goodbye to my small **town**. San Diego, here I come! I have my **ticket** and my seat on the **plane**. I'm next to the window!

THURSDAY AFTERNOON

Now I'm in San Diego, and this is our hotel. These are my friends in front of the hotel.

FRIDAY

Today we're in the **country**, not in the **city**! We're at this cool **ranch** near San Diego. It's a really big **farm**.

SATURDAY

We're at the San Diego Zoo. These birds are funny. They're talking. They say, "Hello. How are you? Hello. How are you?" 🦜🦜🦜

SUNDAY

Now I'm on a **tour** of San Diego Bay. I'm on a **boat** with my friends. They're not listening to the tour guide because they're talking.

A fun **vacation**? I think so. I love it here! 😄

GLOSSARY

tour guide (*n*) this person takes you to a place and tells you about it

2 VOCABULARY: Travel

A 🔊 **2.22** **Listen and repeat the words. Which words are places?**

| boat | country | farm | plane | ranch | ticket | tour | town | vacation |

B ▶ **Now do the vocabulary exercises for 9.1 on page 148.**

C **PAIR WORK** **Which places do you like from Kaitlin's vacation? Which places <u>don't</u> you like? Why?**

3 GRAMMAR: *This* and *These*

A **Circle** the correct answer. Use the sentences in the grammar box to help you.

1 Use *This bird* and *These birds* to talk about **birds around you** / **birds you can't see**.

2 *This* and *these* go **before** / **after** a noun.

3 *This* / *these* goes before a singular noun. *This* / *these* goes before a plural noun.

4 You **can** / **can't** use *this* and *these* at the beginning of a sentence.

> ### *This* and *These*
>
> **This** ticket is expensive.   **These** birds are funny.
>
> We're at **this** cool ranch.   I don't like **these** pictures.

B Kaitlin writes a postcard about a museum. Write *this* or *these* to complete Kaitlin's postcard.

Dear Grandma,

I'm in San Diego! It's great. ¹ _____ postcard shows Balboa Park in the city. The park is very big, and it has 15 museums! ² _____ museums are for art, technology, transportation, and history. We're at the Mingei International Museum right now. You can see it in ³ _____ photo on the right. ⁴ _____ museum is interesting because it has local art – the artists are from ⁵ _____ city. I'm looking at some cool pictures now. ⁶ _____ pictures show places in San Diego. ⁷ _____ artists are *really* good. ⁸ _____ is my favorite room in the museum.

Love, Kaitlin

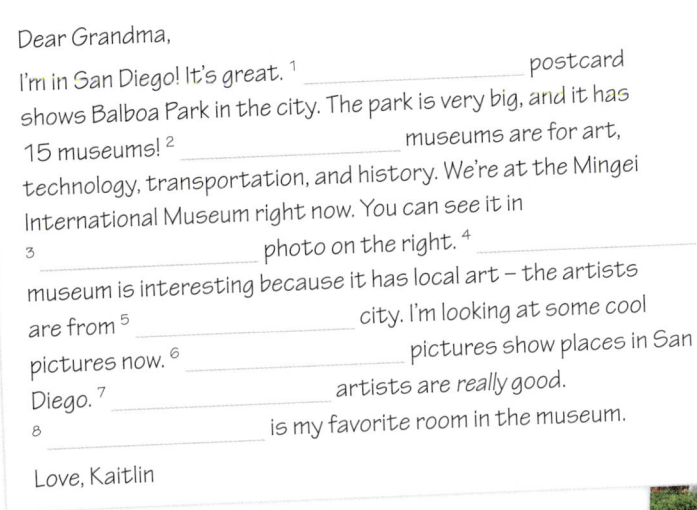

San Diego

C ▶ **Now go to page 137. Look at the grammar chart and do the grammar exercise for 9.1.**

4 SPEAKING

FIND IT

A Choose five pictures on your phone or draw some simple pictures of places you know. Think about the people and places in the pictures.

B PAIR WORK Tell your partner about your pictures.

> This is a picture of my mom and my aunt. They're walking in the country. This hill is very big. What else? This is my favorite aunt. She's...

SAN FRANCISCO, HERE WE COME

LESSON OBJECTIVE
- make travel plans

1 LANGUAGE IN CONTEXT

A 🔊 **2.23** Kaitlin is making a vacation video. Read and listen. Where is she now? Where is she going? How is she going there?

B 🔊 **2.23** Read and listen again. Check (✓) the sentences that are true. Correct the false ones.

☐ 1 The plane is expensive, and the bus is cheap.

☐ 2 You can take a bus to San Francisco at night.

☐ 3 It's Friday night. Kaitlin is sleeping in a hotel.

2 VOCABULARY: Travel arrangements

A 🔊 **2.24** Listen and repeat the sentences. Then match the sentences (a–h) to the pictures (1–8.)

a Stay in a hotel. ___

b Arrive at the airport. ___

c Check in at the airport. ___

d Fly to another airport. You can sleep on the flight. ___

e Leave your house. Ready to travel? ___

f Have a great trip! ___

g Arrive at your destination. ___

h Buy tickets online. ___

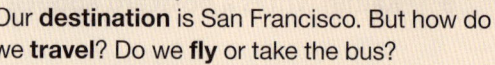

Hello again from San Diego! Today is Tuesday, and we want to **leave** on Friday. Our **destination** is San Francisco. But how do we **travel**? Do we **fly** or take the bus?

Well, the **flight** is two hours. But you have to **arrive** at the **airport** a long time before the flight. You need to **check in** two hours before. So in total, by plane, the **trip** is about five hours. That's not bad. And I like to fly. *But* … the ticket is expensive.

The bus *isn't* expensive. It *is* a long trip – it's 12 hours. But we can take a night bus. And it arrives in San Francisco the next morning. That's good because we don't need to **stay** in a hotel on Friday night.

So, we're taking the bus. We just need to buy our tickets **online**. And then, San Francisco, here we come … on the bus.

B ▶ Now do the vocabulary exercises for 9.2 on page 149.

C [PAIR WORK] Imagine you're going from San Diego to San Francisco. What's a good way to go? Why?

3 GRAMMAR: *like to, want to, need to, have to*

A (Circle) the correct answer. Use the sentences in the grammar box to help you.

1 Use *want to* + verb and *like to* + verb to talk about **necessary things / things you choose to do**.

2 Use *need to* + verb and *have to* + verb to talk about **necessary things / things you choose to do**.

3 After *like to, want to, need to,* and *have to,* use **verb + -ing / verb**.

like to, want to, need to, have to	
I **like to** fly.	She **wants to** take a bus.
You **need to** check in before the flight.	He **has to** buy tickets.
We **want to** leave on Friday.	My mom **likes to** sleep on a flight.

B (Circle) the correct answer to complete the sentences.

1 I always sit by the window because I *need to / like to* look outside. It's interesting!

2 My cell phone isn't old, but I *need to / want to* buy a new one.

3 My wife isn't happy because she *has to / wants to* work this weekend.

4 On Fridays, we *like to / need to* watch TV after dinner.

5 He starts work at 6:30, so he *needs to / wants to* get up really early.

C ▶ **Now go to page 138. Look at the grammar chart and do the grammar exercise for 9.2.**

D PAIR WORK Write <u>four</u> sentences that are true for you. Use *like to, want to, need to,* and *have to.* Then compare your sentences with a partner and check your accuracy.

✓ **ACCURACY** CHECK

Use *to* with *want, like, need* and *have* when they are before another verb.

I like fly. ✗
I like to fly. ✓

4 SPEAKING

A Work alone. Imagine you have to take a trip for one of these reasons: vacation, work, or to visit family. Where do you want to go? How do you want to travel: on a bus, a train, or a plane? For ideas, watch Larissa's video.

B PAIR WORK Tell your partner about your trip. Talk about the things you need to do for your trip.

REAL STUDENT *Do you want to travel the same way as Larissa?*

I have to take a trip for work.

Where do you have to go?

Buenos Aires, and I want to go by plane. I like to fly.

You can buy your ticket online …

THEY'RE TWO FOR $15

1 FUNCTIONAL LANGUAGE

A 🔊 **2.25** Andy arrives at the airport in Mexico City. Read and listen. What does he want to buy? What does he want to drink? What place does he ask about?

🔊 **2.25 Audio script**

Andy	Hello. I need a travel guide for Mexico City. **Where are the travel guides?**
Clerk	Sorry, can you say that again?
Andy	Travel guides – where are the travel guides?
Clerk	Oh, OK. They're here, with the books and magazines.
Andy	OK. **How much is that?**
Clerk	It's $9.99.
Andy	Great. I need to buy a travel guide for Guadalajara, too. **Is it the same price, $9.99?**
Clerk	Yes, it is. But good news! **They're two for $15.**
Andy	Great! I want both, please. Hey, **what time does the café open?** I really need some coffee.
Clerk	**It opens in about 10 minutes.**
Andy	OK. **And where is the men's restroom?**
Clerk	It's over there, next to the café. But first you need to buy your books!

INSIDER ENGLISH

People often say *restroom* in public places and *bathroom* in people's homes. *Restroom* is more polite.

At an airport:
Where is the men's restroom?

At a friend's house:
Sorry, where's your bathroom?

GLOSSARY

travel guide (*n*) a book with information about where to go and what to see in a city or country

B Complete the chart with expressions in **bold** from the conversation above.

Asking for information	Giving information
1 _____ the travel guides?	6 _____ $9.99.
2 _____ that?	7 _____ $15.
3 _____ , $9.99?	8 _____ about 10 minutes.
4 _____ the café open?	
5 _____ the men's restroom?	

C 🔊 **2.26** Complete the conversations with words from the chart above. Listen and check.

1 A Excuse me. _____ is this smartwatch?

B _____ $125.49.

A What about this big smartwatch? Is it the _____ ?

B No, it isn't. _____ $149.00.

2 A _____ flight 248 arrive?

B It arrives _____ 30 minutes.

A OK, thanks. Oh, and _____ the women's _____ ?

B It's over there.

2 REAL-WORLD STRATEGY

ASKING SOMEONE TO REPEAT SOMETHING

To hear information again, ask, *Sorry, can you say that again?* or *Can you repeat that, please?*

Andy   *Where are the travel guides?*

Clerk   *Sorry, can you say that again?*

A   Read the information in the box. What question does the clerk ask? Why?

B   🔊 **2.27** Listen to a conversation. Does the woman understand the man the first time? What question does she ask? How much is the cell phone?

3 PRONUNCIATION: Saying prices

A   🔊 **2.28** Listen and repeat the prices. Where does the speaker put stress in each price?

1 $6.19 / $6.90   3 $17.30 / $70.13   5 $2.16 / $2.60

2 $15 / $50   4 $19 / $90   6 $14 / $40

B   🔊 **2.29** Listen and write the prices. Then practice the conversation with a partner.

A I love that picture! How much is it?

B It's $_____ .

A $_____ ! That's cheap!

B No, it's $_____ .

A Oh …

C   PAIR WORK   Work with a partner. Ask to buy your friend's cell phone, bag, or Student's Book. Make a mistake with the price. Use the conversation in exercise 3B for an example. Then change roles.

4 SPEAKING

FIND IT

PAIR WORK   Imagine you want to buy something. Look at the items below, or go online and find an item. Take turns being the customer. Ask for information, and ask the store clerk to repeat something. Then change roles.

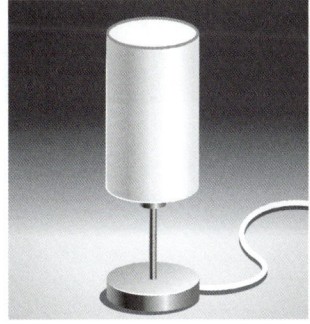

$29.99, or two for $50 $6, or two for $10.50 $13, or two for $20 $45, or two for $79

> Excuse me. How much is this mug?

> It's $6, or two for $10.50.

> Sorry, can you repeat that, please?

A GREAT DESTINATION

1 READING

A RECOGNIZE TEXT TYPE **Read the text. What is it from?**

☐ a travel guide   ☐ an email   ☐ a review   ☐ a student's homework

✈ **Travel**Smart PLACES TO GO **NEAR PUNO**

TAQUILE ISLAND

Taquile Island is in Lake Titicaca in Peru. You can see mountains in Bolivia from the island. About 2,000 people live on this interesting island.

TRANSPORTATION

You have to take a boat to the island from Puno. You can go with a tour company, or you can get a local boat. You are on the boat for about three hours. There are no cars on the island, so you have to walk after you arrive. It's a 40-minute walk to the town, and you can see a lot of nature on the way.

WHERE TO STAY

There are a small number of hotels on Taquile Island. You need to reserve a room before your trip. Prices are from $20 to $60 a night. You can also stay with a local family for about $9.

THINGS TO DO

● You can see dances in the town.

● You can eat at a restaurant or have lunch with a local family.

● The market has a lot of things to see, buy, and eat.

GLOSSARY

local (*adj*) from the nearby area or neighborhood

reserve (a room) (*v*) book or pay for a room before you travel to a place

18

B SCAN **Find the numbers in the text. What do these numbers mean?**

2,000   three   40 $20 to $60 $9

C READ FOR DETAILS **Read the text again. Circle the correct answers.**

1 Taquile Island *is* / *isn't* in Bolivia.

2 You *can* / *can't* get a boat to the island.

3 You *can* / *can't* drive on the island.

4 There are *no* / *some* hotels on the island.

5 There *are* / *aren't* restaurants on the island.

6 You *can* / *can't* meet local people.

D PAIR WORK THINK CRITICALLY **Why do people like to go to Taquile Island? Do you want to go there? Why or why not? Give examples from the text to explain your answer.**

2 WRITING

A Read Cameron's review of Taquile Island. What does he say <u>not</u> to do?

DestinationsNow

About | Hotels | Restaurants | Search

Taquile Island
Lake Titicaca, Puno, Peru

Reviews (365) — Write a review

Very good		673
Good		575
OK		6
Bad		0
Very bad		0

Search review topics

★★★★★ 3 weeks ago

Cameron T.

You have to see Taquile Island!

This island is really nice. It's not very big. There is only one town on the island. There are a lot of small homes on the hills, and there's a lot of nature. I like to walk, and you have to walk a lot on Taquile. Walk to the top of the island and see the ocean. You can see Peru on one side and Bolivia on the other side. You can even see snow on the mountains in Bolivia. Don't take a tour with a travel company. Take a local boat and stay with a family. The people are very friendly. You don't need to eat at the restaurants in town. The food is OK, but the family gives you a great breakfast, lunch, and dinner. Talk with the family. You can learn a lot about Taquile this way. Don't forget your camera. You can take a lot of pictures of this wonderful place!

GLOSSARY
wonderful (*adj*) really good

B **WRITING SKILLS** Read the information about imperative verbs below. Then <u>underline</u> all the sentences beginning with an imperative verb in Cameron's review in exercise 2A.

You can use imperative verbs to give someone advice. An imperative verb is a verb with no subject (e.g. *he, she*).

+ **Walk** to the top of the island and see the ocean.

– **Don't take** a tour with a travel company.

WRITE IT

REGISTER CHECK

People often use imperative verbs in informal writing to give advice.

In a website review: *Walk to the top of the island*.

People usually use verb forms with subjects in formal writing.

In a travel guide: *You can walk to the top of the island*.

C Choose a place for people to visit in your area. Write a review of the place. Say what people can do and see. Use imperative verbs to give advice. Use Cameron's review in exercise 2A for an example.

D **PAIR WORK** Read your partner's review. Do you want to visit your partner's place? Why or why not?

TIME TO SPEAK
Vacation plans

A **DISCUSS** Look at the pictures. What do you think these people like to do on vacation? For each person, say <u>three</u> things. Compare your ideas with a partner. Find a new idea for each person.

Jim

Minako

Carter

B **DECIDE** Work in pairs. Choose Jim, Minako, or Carter. Imagine they are coming to your country on vacation for two weeks. What do you think they want to do? Make a list of things to do and places to go.

C **PREPARE** Imagine you are helping this person plan a vacation. Look at your list from exercise B. What do you need to do? Make a plan.

D **AGREE** Work in groups: Group Jim, Group Minako, or Group Carter. Present your plan. Which plan is your group's favorite?

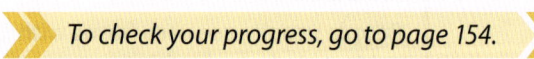

To check your progress, go to page 154.

USEFUL PHRASES

DISCUSS
I think Jim/Minako/Carter likes to … on vacation.
What do you think Jim/Minako/Carter likes to do?
My three ideas for Jim are …
I agree. / I disagree.
Let's think of one new idea for Minako.

DECIDE
A good thing to do / place to go is …
On the first day, he/she can …

AGREE
We're planning a vacation for …
This is our plan.
Our favorite plan is … because it's interesting/fun/nice.

REVIEW 3 (UNITS 7–9)

1 VOCABULARY

A **Write the words in the chart. There are <u>five</u> words or phrases for each group.**

airport	clean my room	do homework	paint	take a break
be on the subway	company	draw	play the guitar	take the bus
brush my hair	dance	have a meeting	sing	do the dishes
check in	destination	office	take a bath	workers

Activities around the house	Transportation/Travel	Skills	Work

B **Add <u>one</u> more word or phrase to each group in exercise 1A.**

2 GRAMMAR

A **Put the words in the correct order to make sentences.**

1 my / right / cleaning / I'm / room / now. _____

2 aren't / homework. / The / doing / children / their _____

3 bus? / Is / waiting / she / a / for _____

4 days. / hard / is / these / father / My / working _____

5 watching / TV / not / right now. / They're _____

6 you / these / reading / What / days? / books / are _____

B [PAIR WORK] **Tell a partner two or three things you are doing these days. For example, what you're reading or watching on TV, what classes you're taking, or what games/sports you're playing.**

C **Complete the sentences with *can* or *can't*.**

1 My brother usually goes out for dinner because he _____ cook.

2 I _____ swim really well. I usually swim in the evening after work.

3 Juan _____ speak four languages: Spanish, Portuguese, French, and Italian.

4 My sister _____ skateboard, and she doesn't want to learn.

5 I _____ drive a car. It's easy.

6 My grandfather _____ use a computer. He doesn't have one, and he doesn't want one.

D [PAIR WORK] **Talk to a partner. Say <u>two</u> things you can do and <u>two</u> things you can't do.**

3 SPEAKING

A   **PAIR WORK** **You're going to play a guessing game with your partner. Follow the instructions.**

1 Work alone. Choose one of these places, but <u>don't</u> tell your partner: in a room at home, in an office, in a classroom, on a train or a bus, in a car. Now, imagine you're in the place.

2 Talk to your partner. Say what you can and can't do in the place. Say what you're doing there now.

3 Your partner guesses the place. You can say *"Yes."* or *"No."*

> I can sleep here, and I can use my phone. I can't cook here, but I can go places. Right now, I'm studying here.

> Is it a classroom?

> No!

B   **Write about your partner's place in exercise 3A. Describe what he/she can and can't do there.**

4 FUNCTIONAL LANGUAGE

A   **(Circle) the correct answers.**

Robert   Hi, Marina! ¹ *I'm / It's* Robert.

Marina   Hey, Robert! How are you ² *do / doing*?

Robert   Not ³ *bad / fine*, thanks. And you?

Marina   ⁴ *I'm / It's* fine. What are you doing these days?

Robert   Well, I'm planning a trip to Rio for five days.

Marina   ⁵ *Oh, wow! / Oh no!* That's great!

Robert   Yeah, and the hotel's a good price.

Marina   Really? ⁶ *How much / When* is it?

Robert $189.99 a night.

Marina   ⁷ *I don't think / I think* that's a good price. That's really, really expensive!

Robert   ⁸ *I think / I think so* it's good. ⁹ *I mean / I say*, it's a five-star hotel.

Marina   ¹⁰ *Oh. / Oh no!* ¹¹ *Where / What* is it?

Robert   In Copacabana.

5 SPEAKING

A   **PAIR WORK** **Choose one of the situations below. Talk to a partner. Have a conversation.**

1 Start a telephone conversation. Ask how your partner is and what he/she is doing these days. Look at page 70 for useful language.

> Hi, Ji-un. How are you?

2 Talk about things people do in unusual offices. Give your opinion about these things. Look at page 80 for useful language.

> In some offices, you can play computer games. I don't think that's a good idea. I mean, people need to work!

3 You're at an airport and need information about prices, locations, and times. Look at page 90 for useful language.

> Excuse me. How much are these travel guides?

B   **PAIR WORK** **Change roles and repeat the situation.**

UNIT OBJECTIVES

- make outdoor plans for the weekend
- discuss what clothes to wear for different trips
- suggest plans for evening activities
- write an online invitation
- plan and present a fun weekend in your city

START SPEAKING

A   Look at the picture. Imagine you're doing this.
    Say things you can do to get ready before you do it.

B   Do you have big plans for the future? What are they?
    For ideas, watch Larissa's video.

REAL STUDENT

Are your plans the same as Larissa's?

10.1 WHITE NIGHTS

LESSON OBJECTIVE
- make outdoor plans for the weekend

Midnight in St. Petersburg

To: sofiaperez@mymail.com
From: averin.yana@grabmail.org
Subject: Your trip

Reply Forward

Hi Sofia,

You're going to be here next weekend! I'm very happy because you're going to see St. Petersburg during the White Nights. It's light for about 24 hours in June. We live *outside* – all day and *all night*.

So, here's the plan. On Friday evening, I'm going to **meet** you at the airport and then **take** you out to dinner. We're going to **eat** outside at Marketplace. It's my favorite restaurant.

On Saturday, we're going to **look at** art at the Street Art Museum. And, of course, we can **go** shopping on Nevsky Prospect. And then in the evening, we're going to **get together** with some of my friends in Kirov Park. We can **take** a walk in the park, and then we're going to **have** a picnic – at midnight!

What else do you want to do? I'm not going to be home tonight, but we can talk tomorrow.

See you soon!

Yana

GLOSSARY
light (*adj*) the sun is in the sky

1 LANGUAGE IN CONTEXT

A PAIR WORK Look at the picture. Where is it? What time is it? What's unusual about it?

B Read the email and answer the questions.
1 Why is Yana happy?
2 What are the "White Nights"?
3 When does Yana want to talk to Sofia?

2 VOCABULARY: Going out

A 🔊 2.30 Find these verbs in the email. Then complete the phrases with the verbs. Listen and check.

eat   get together   go   have   look at   meet   take (2x)

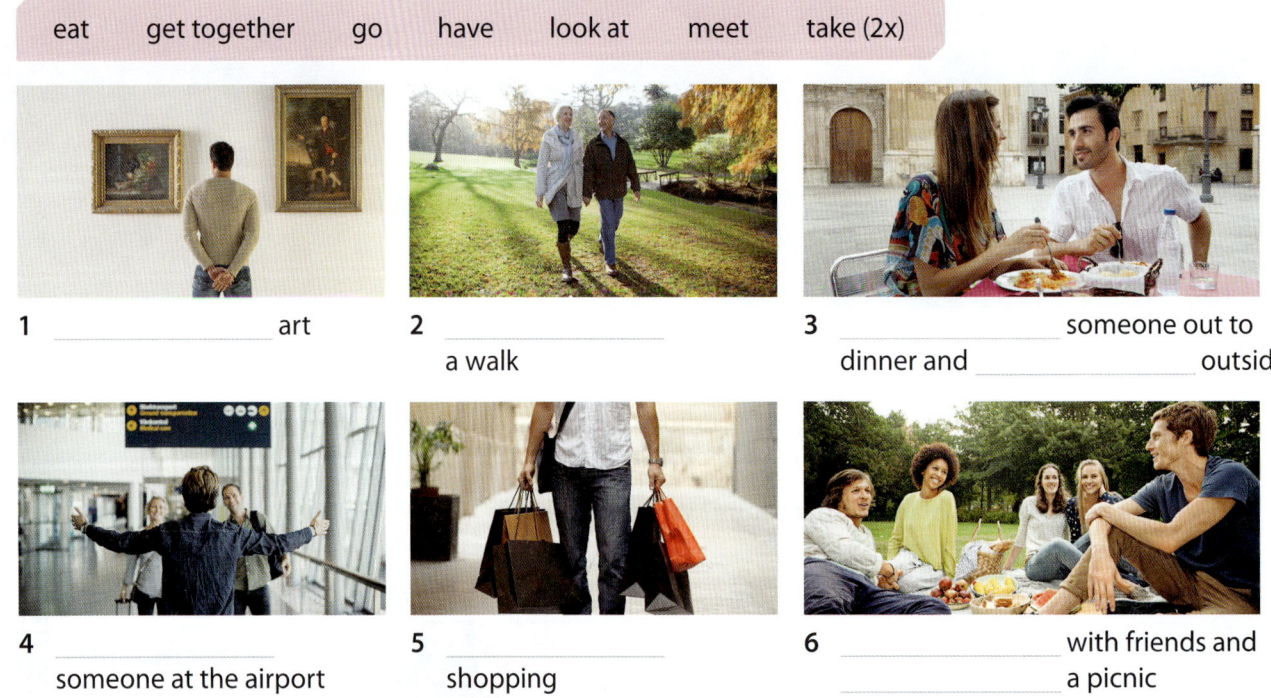

1 _____ art

2 _____ a walk

3 _____ someone out to dinner and _____ outside

4 _____ someone at the airport

5 _____ shopping

6 _____ with friends and _____ a picnic

B ▶ Now do the vocabulary exercises for 10.1 on page 149.

C GROUP WORK How often do you do the activities in exercise 2A? Tell your group.

3 GRAMMAR: Statements with *be going to*

A (Circle) the correct answer. Use the sentences in the grammar box to help you.

1 Use *be going to* to talk about **things you're doing right now / future plans**.

2 Make future statements with *be going to* + **a verb / a noun**.

Statements with *be going to*

I**'m going to be** home tomorrow.

It**'s going to be** light all night.

You**'re going to meet** me at the airport.

We**'re going to get together** with some of my friends.

I**'m not going to be** home tonight.

It **isn't going to be** light all night.

My friends **aren't going to go** shopping.

They**'re not going to eat** outside this weekend.

B **Complete the sentences with *be going to* and the affirmative or negative form of the verb in parentheses ( ).**

1 I _____ (be) home tomorrow. I have to work at the office.

2 My parents _____ (take) me to lunch on Saturday. They're busy.

3 My friends and I _____ (go) on a trip to Rio next year. We have our tickets!

4 I _____ (study) a lot next week. I have an important test.

5 My friend _____ (meet) me tonight. She's sick.

C [PAIR WORK] **Change the sentences in exercise 3B so they're true for you. Then compare with a partner.**

> I'm not going to be home tomorrow. I have to go to college.

D ▶ **Now go to page 138. Look at the grammar chart and do the grammar exercise for 10.1.**

4 SPEAKING

A [PAIR WORK] **What can you do outside in your city? Make a list.**

> We can eat outside at a lot of restaurants.

> True. And we can watch movies outside.

B [PAIR WORK] **Make outdoor plans with your partner for next weekend. Then share your plans with the class.**

> Next Saturday, we're going have a picnic in …

10.2 BUT IT'S SUMMER THERE!

1 VOCABULARY: Clothes; seasons

A 🔊 **2.31** Listen and repeat the clothes. Then look at the people in your class. How many of the clothes can you see?

B 🔊 **2.32** **PAIR WORK** Look at the seasons below. Listen and repeat. What seasons do you have where you live? When are they?

spring

summer

fall

winter

dry season

rainy season

hat

pants

shirt

coat

shorts

dress

shoes

skirt

jeans

sweater

T-shirt

boots

C ▶ Now do the vocabulary exercises for 10.2 on page 149.

2 LANGUAGE IN CONTEXT

A 🔊 **2.33** Read and listen. Sofia and her friend discuss Sofia's trip to St. Petersburg. What clothes do they talk about?

🔊 **2.33 Audio script**

Rena So, are you ready for your trip? What clothes are you going to take?

Sofia Yeah, I am! I'm going to take a big **coat**, and I need to buy a **hat**.

Rena Really? But it's **summer** there!

Sofia Yes, but it's Russia, not Florida! It's not hot in the summer.

Rena True, but it's not *cold*. So, are you going to take **pants** and some **sweaters**?

Sofia Yes, I am. No. I don't know. I usually wear **shorts** in the summer here, but … Oh, I know! I can take my **fall** or **spring** pants.

Rena Good idea. And what are you going to wear on your feet?

Sofia I need some new **shoes**. We're going to walk outside a lot. Or maybe **boots**.

Rena When are you going to leave? I mean, are you *really* ready for this trip?

INSIDER ENGLISH

You can say, *Oh, I know!* when you think of a good idea or an answer to a problem.

Oh, I know! I can take my fall or winter pants.

GLOSSARY

wear (v) have clothes on your body

100

B PAIR WORK **What season is it now? What clothes do you usually wear? For ideas, watch Anderson's video.**

REAL STUDENT

Are your answers the same as Anderson's?

3 GRAMMAR: Questions with *be going to*

A Circle **the correct answers. Use the sentences in the grammar box to help you.**

1 A *yes/no* question with *be going to* begins with **Am, Is,** or **Are** / **What, Where,** or **When**.

2 For information questions with *be going to*, put the question word **before** / **after** *is, are,* or *am*.

Questions with *be going to*

Yes/no questions

Are you **going to take** some sweaters?   Yes, I **am**. / No, I'**m not**.

Is Sofia **going to see** a friend?   Yes, she **is**. / No, she'**s not**.

Information questions

What are you **going to take**?

When are you **going to leave**?

Where is Sofia **going to go**?

Who are you **going to meet**?

B **Put the words in the correct order to make questions.**

1 are / going to / this weekend? / What / you / do

2 study / Are / tonight? / going to / you

3 have / you / What / for dinner? / are / going to

4 on TV? / going to / are / watch / you / What

5 tomorrow? / go / you / are / Where / going to

6 going to / your / next week? / see / Are / friends / you

C ▶ **Now go to page 139. Look at the grammar chart and do the grammar exercise for 10.2.**

D PAIR WORK **Read the Accuracy check box. Then ask and answer the questions in exercise 3B with a partner.**

✔ **ACCURACY** CHECK

Do not use *be going to* in short answers.
Are you going to wear a dress to the party?
No, I'm not ~~going to.~~ ✗
Yes, I am. ✓

4 SPEAKING

A **Look at the trips. Choose two, and plan what clothes you're going to take with you.**

- A two-week trip to Miami, Florida, in the summer. (29°C / 84°F)
- A one-week trip to Vienna, Austria, in the winter. (2°C / 36°F)
- A five-day trip to Vancouver, Canada, in the spring. (20°C / 68°F)
- A two-week trip to Manaus, Brazil, in the rainy season. (30°C / 86°F)

B PAIR WORK **Ask questions about your partners' trips.**

Where are you going to go?

First, I'm going to go to Miami this summer.

Oh, great! What clothes are you going to take?

101

10.3 LET'S MEET AT THE HOTEL

LESSON OBJECTIVE
- suggest plans for evening activities

1 FUNCTIONAL LANGUAGE

A Jonathan is in Mexico City for a meeting with his coworker, Antonio. They're making plans to go out in the evening. What do you think they are saying?

B 🔊 **2.34** Read and listen. Where are Antonio and Jonathan going to have dinner? Where are they going to meet? What time are they going to meet?

🔊 **2.34 Audio script**

Antonio	So, Jonathan, **why don't we go out tonight?**
Jonathan	**OK, sounds good.**
Antonio	Do you like Mexican food?
Jonathan	I love it! Are there any good Mexican restaurants in town?
Antonio	Um, in Mexico City? Yeah, I know one or two places!
Jonathan	I'm sure you do!
Antonio	There's a very good restaurant near your hotel. Why don't we go there?
Jonathan	**Good idea.**
Antonio	So **let's meet at the hotel**.
Jonathan	OK. What time? Eight o'clock?
Antonio	Um … **I'm sorry, but I can't**. How about eight-thirty?
Jonathan	**Yes, sure.**

C Complete the chart with expressions in **bold** from the conversation above.

Making suggestions	Accepting suggestions	Refusing suggestions
1 _____ go out tonight? 2 _____ meet at the hotel.	OK, 3 _____ good. Good 4 _____ . Yes, 5 _____ .	I'm sorry, 6 _____ . Sorry, I'm busy.

D 🔊 **2.35** Complete the conversations with words from exercise 1C. Listen and check. Then practice with a partner.

1 A _____ take a break.
   B OK, sounds _____ .

2 A _____ have lunch?
   B _____ , but I can't.

3 A Coffee?
   B _____ idea.

2 REAL-WORLD STRATEGY

SAYING WHY YOU CAN'T DO SOMETHING

After you say, *I'm sorry, but I can't*, you can give a reason with *I have to*.

Jonathan   *What time? Eight o'clock?*

Antonio   *I'm sorry, but I can't. I have to go home first. How about eight-thirty?*

A   **Read the information in the box above. Why can't Antonio meet at eight o'clock?**

B   🔊 **2.36   Listen to a conversation. What are the man and woman going to do, and when?**

C   🔊 **2.36   Listen again. Why can't the woman have a meeting on Monday?**

D   ▶ **PAIR WORK   Student A: Go to page 158. Student B: Go to page 160. Follow the instructions.**

3 PRONUNCIATION: Saying the letter *s*

A   🔊 **2.37   Listen and repeat. How is the letter *s* different in the words?**

/s/   **s**orry   /z/   bu**s**y

B   🔊 **2.38   Read and say the words below. Which sound does the letter *s* have? Write /s/ or /z/. Some words have two sounds. Then listen and check.**

1 restaurants	3 tickets	5 station	7 jeans
2 movies	4 shoes	6 season	8 shorts

C   🔊 **2.39   PAIR WORK   Listen and repeat the sentences. Focus on the /s/ and /z/ sounds. Then practice the sentences with a partner.**

1   Are there any re**s**taurant**s** in town?   3   Are there any movie**s** on TV tonight?

2   I'm **s**orry, but I can't. I'm bu**s**y tonight.   4   Why don't we get ticket**s** at the **s**tation?

4 SPEAKING

PAIR WORK   Imagine your partner is in your town or city on a business or study trip. He/She is staying at a hotel in the city. Suggest something to do in the evening. Also suggest a place to go and a time to meet. Then change roles.

> Let's go out this evening.

> Why don't we go to a restaurant? Do you like Italian food?

> Good idea.

A 24-HOUR CITY

1 LISTENING

A **PAIR WORK** Look at the city in the pictures on pages 104 and 105. What do you think you can you do there?

B 🔊 **2.40** **LISTEN FOR DETAILS** Listen to the start of a TV travel show about Montevideo. Which <u>two</u> cities does the woman talk about? Which <u>two</u> neighborhoods in Montevideo does she talk about?

C 🔊 **2.40** **LISTEN FOR EXAMPLES** Listen again. Check (✓) the places the woman says.

☐ restaurants   ☐ places to go dancing   ☐ hotels
☐ the ocean   ☐ the beach   ☐ museums

D **PAIR WORK** **THINK CRITICALLY** The woman says, "This really is a day-and-night city." Look at the places in exercise 1C. Where do people usually go: in the day? at night? at night *and* in the day?

2 PRONUNCIATION: Listening for *going to*

A 🔊 **2.41** Listen to the sentences. Do you hear *going to* or *gonna*? (Circle) the correct words.
1 I'm not *going to* / *gonna* go dancing now.
2 We're *going to* / *gonna* walk by the ocean in Old City.

B 🔊 **2.42** Listen. What do you hear? (Circle) *going to* or *gonna*.
1 *going to* / *gonna*   3 *going to* / *gonna*
2 *going to* / *gonna*   4 *going to* / *gonna*

C People often use *gonna* in informal conversations. (Circle) the correct answer.
People usually say *gonna* when they are **at work** / **talking to friends**.

A   **Read the online invitation. What does Ramon say his friends can wear? Which night is a surprise?**

Reply   Forward

| From: | Ramon |
| Subject: | Montevideo Nights |

MESSAGE FROM RAMON

EVENT	Montevideo Nights
HOST	Ramon
WHEN	Friday and Saturday, December 19–20
WHERE	Montevideo, Uruguay
MEET	Hotel Central, Friday, December 19 at 9:30 p.m.

This is a city that never sleeps. *You're* not going to sleep, either! ⭐🌙 😃 Meet me at the front door of the hotel. Don't be late! And don't eat dinner first because we're going to eat at a nice restaurant in the Pocitos neighborhood. Then we're going to go dancing – all night! Early in the morning, about 5:00 a.m., we're going to watch the sunrise at the beach and then go for a morning walk by the ocean. It's a great place for a picnic – a breakfast picnic. 😃 And then why don't we play soccer on the beach? A lot of people play soccer on the beach in the summer. You can wear shorts and a T-shirt, but a sweater is good for the early morning. On Saturday night, we're going to … well, it's a surprise! 😲 See you Friday night!

GLOSSARY

sunrise (*n*) early in the morning, when the sun is first in the sky
surprise (*n*) something you don't know about

B   **WRITING SKILLS** **Look at the contractions in two of Ramon's sentences below. Then underline all 10 contractions in his message. Work with a partner and say the full forms.**

U̲n̲d̲e̲r̲l̲i̲n̲e̲ not going to sleep, either! (*You're = You are*)

D̲o̲n̲'t̲ be late! (*Don't = Do not*)

REGISTER CHECK

Many speakers of English use contractions in informal writing. In formal writing, people often use the full forms.

 **WRITE IT**

FIND IT

C   **Plan an exciting day or night out for your friends. You can look online for ideas. Then write an online invitation. Use Ramon's invitation for an example. Describe where you are going to go and what you are going to do. Use contractions.**

D   GROUP WORK **Read the other invitations in your group. Which events do you want to go to? Why?**

TIME TO SPEAK
48 hours in your city

A　**PREPARE**　Look at the pictures. Can you do these things in your country? When can you do them? Think about seasons, days, and times of day.

B　**RESEARCH**　Work with a partner. Choose a season or a month. Think of fun things to do in your city in that season/month during the day, at night, and outside. Write a list.

C　**AGREE**　Plan a fun weekend (48 hours) in your city. Choose activities from exercise B. Make a plan for Saturday and Sunday.

D　**DISCUSS**　Work with another pair and compare your plans. Ask and answer questions about their plan.

E　**PRESENT**　With your partner, present your 48-hour plan to the class. Which plan do you want to do?

To check your progress, go to page 155.

USEFUL PHRASES

RESEARCH

Let's talk about the summer / February / the rainy season.

What fun things can we do during the day? at night? outside?

DISCUSS

We're going to have breakfast in the park.

Are you going to have a picnic?

PRESENT

We're planning a fun weekend in (season/month).

First, we're going to …

On Saturday/Sunday, …

UNIT OBJECTIVES

- describe people, places, and things in the past
- talk about colors and memories
- talk about movies and actors
- write an email about things you keep from your past
- talk about TV shows from your childhood

COLORFUL MEMORIES

11

START SPEAKING

A Look at the picture. Where is the boy? How old is the boy now?

B Is the boy happy? Why or why not?

C Talk about a happy time in your life. For ideas, watch Felipe's video.

REAL STUDENT

What time does Felipe talk about? Do you remember the same time?

LESSON OBJECTIVE
- describe people, places, and things in the past

1 LANGUAGE IN CONTEXT

A Mason writes about two old pictures from his past. Read his posts and the comments. (Circle) the topics he writes about.

his school	his first job
the season	a toy
his family	his favorite food

B Read again. Check (✓) the sentences that are true. Correct the false ones.

☐ 1 Flashback Friday is for pictures from the past.

☐ 2 The yard is at Mason's parents' house.

☐ 3 Bethany is Mason's friend now.

☐ 4 Mason drives a car these days.

2 VOCABULARY: Describing people, places, and things

A 🔊 **2.43** Listen and repeat the adjectives in **bold**. Which adjectives in Mason's posts describe people, places, and things?

Mason Clark It's Flashback Friday! Here are two of my favorite memories from 2009. I was eight. This was in the summer. I was with my sister, and we were on vacation at my grandparents' house. My parents weren't there. It was **exciting**! #flashbackfriday #2009 #summervacation

Mason Clark
Bethany Clark

Fay L. Wright You were really **cute**!

Bert Chow Your grandparents' yard was **beautiful**!

Mason Clark Yeah, it was **wonderful**. It was usually **quiet**, but not in the summer. We were **noisy** kids!

Mason Clark And this was my old go-kart. My grandpa made it for me. Well, it wasn't old in 2009 – it was **new** then! It was **slow**, but to me, at eight, it was really **fast** and exciting. #go-kart #2009 #bestgrandparents

Sam Lopez My go-kart was **awful**, but yours is great.

Bethany Clark Hey, Mason is still driving it today! 😂

Mason Clark Don't listen to my sister! I have a real, *fast* car now. 😊

👍 13 ❤️ 2

GLOSSARY
memories (n) things you think about from your past
yard (n) the outdoor area in front of or behind a house

new shoes

cute dog

wonderful vacation

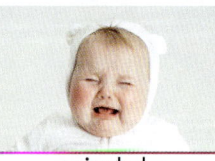
noisy baby

fast car

exciting book

beautiful day

awful day

quiet baby

slow car

B ▶ Now do the vocabulary exercises for 11.1 on page 150.

C GROUP WORK Think about a person, place, or thing from your past. Describe it to your group. Use the adjectives in exercise 2A. For ideas, watch Anderson's video.

REAL STUDENT

Is Anderson's memory happy? Is your memory happy, too?

3 GRAMMAR: Statements with *was* and *were*

A (Circle) the correct answer. Use the sentences in the grammar box to help you.

1 Use *was* and *were* to talk about people, places, or things in the **past** / **future**.

2 *Was* and *were* are the simple past forms of **go** / **be**.

3 *Was* and *were* are **affirmative** / **negative**.

4 *Wasn't* and *weren't* are **affirmative** / **negative**.

Statements with *was* and *were*

I **was** in the yard.   My parents **weren't** there.

We **were** on vacation.   It **wasn't** old.

B Read another Flashback Friday post. Complete the post with *was*, *wasn't*, *were*, or *weren't*.

Ethan Collins
March 14 at 3:37 p.m.

I remember a visit to my uncle's farm in August 1998. It ¹ _____ a big farm – just a nice, small one. There ² _____ a lot of animals, only ten or fifteen. They ³ _____ farm animals, not pets, so they ⁴ _____ friendly, but my uncle's dog ⁵ _____ really nice. He ⁶ _____ only two or three, so he ⁷ _____ very old, but he ⁸ _____ smart. His real name ⁹ _____ Jake, but my name for him ¹⁰ _____ "Fluffy Duffy." It's an awful name, but I ¹¹ _____ seven at the time, and to me, Fluffy Duffy ¹² _____ a beautiful name! We ¹³ _____ great friends.
#flashbackfriday #1998 #bestfriend

👍 Like   💬 Comment   ➤ Share

👍 35   ❤ 8

Fluffy Duffy

GLOSSARY
remember (*v*) think about something from the past

C   ▶ Now go to page 139. Look at the grammar chart and do the grammar exercise for 11.1.

D   PAIR WORK   Write sentences with *was* or *were*. Use the words in parentheses ( ). Then check your accuracy. Which sentences are true for you?

When I was a child …

1 (My friends / wonderful) _____ .

2 (My hometown / beautiful) _____ .

3 (My brother's car / awful) _____ .

4 (My cat / really cute) _____ .

✓ **ACCURACY** CHECK

Do **not** forget to use *was*, *wasn't*, *were*, or *weren't* before adjectives when describing the past.

He cute. ✗
He was cute. ✓

4 SPEAKING

A Choose one or two of your memories. Think about the ideas below or your own ideas. Write notes.

ages   animals   the people   the place   the season   the year   things

B   PAIR WORK   Talk about your memories. You can begin, *"I remember …"*

I remember my sister's birthday party. It was July 2006. She was thirteen. The party was very noisy, and …

11.2 OUR OLD PHONE WAS WHITE

LESSON OBJECTIVE
- talk about colors and memories

1 LANGUAGE IN CONTEXT

A   **PAIR WORK** Look at the picture of the child. Describe it with one word.

B   🔊 **2.44** Emilio talks to his wife, Paula. Read and listen. Where was Emilio in the picture? Which rooms does Paula remember?

🔊 2.44 Audio script

Emilio Here's another picture of me.

Paula Cute! How old were you?

Emilio I don't know. Two?

Paula And where were you? Were you at home?

Emilio No, I wasn't, because our phone was **black**. Hmm … so where was the **green** phone? Oh, yeah! It was at my grandparents' house, in the kitchen.

Paula Hey, I remember our old phone, too. It was **white**.

Emilio Wow, you remember the color, too! Was it big? Our old phone was *really* big.

Paula Yeah, it was. I remember a lot! The phone was in the living room, next to the couch. The couch was **brown**. And the living room walls were **orange**. Oh, yeah, and my bedroom walls were **pink** and green. Yuck! It's really easy to remember the colors of things – even ugly colors!

GLOSSARY
ugly (*adj*) not nice to look at

C   🔊 **2.44** Read and listen again. Then answer the questions.

1   How many phones does Emilio talk about?

2   Paula remembers the color of her phone, living room walls, bedroom walls – and which other thing?

INSIDER ENGLISH

You can say, *Oh, yeah,* when you remember something.

Where was the green phone? **Oh, yeah!** *It was at my grandmother's house.*

Oh, yeah, *and my bedroom walls were pink and green.*

2 VOCABULARY: Colors

A   🔊 **2.45** **PAIR WORK** Listen and repeat the colors. Which colors are in the conversation above? What's your favorite color?

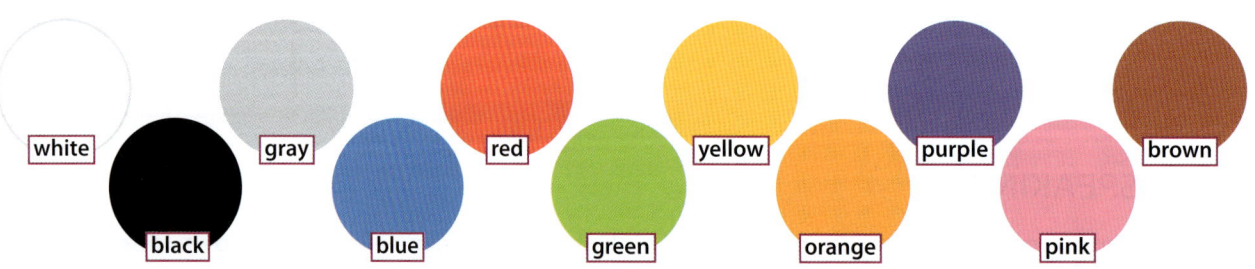

white   gray   red   yellow   purple   brown
black   blue   green   orange   pink

B   ▶ Now do the vocabulary exercises for 11.2 on page 150.

C   **PAIR WORK** Tell your partner the colors of <u>two</u> things from your home.

3 GRAMMAR: Questions with *was* and *were*

A **Circle the correct answers. Use the questions in the grammar box to help you.**

1 In *yes/no* questions, *was* and *were* go at the **beginning** / **end** of the question.

2 In information questions, *was* and *were* go **before** / **after** the question word(s) (for example, *How old* and *When*).

Questions with *was* and *were*

Yes/no questions	Information questions
Were you at home?	How old **were** you?
No, I **wasn't**.	I **was** two.
Was the phone in the kitchen?	What color **were** the walls?
Yes, it **was**.	They **were** orange.

B PAIR WORK **Put the words in the correct order to make questions. Then ask and answer the questions with a partner.**

1 color / your old phone? / was / What

2 was / the phone? / Where

3 in the kitchen? / the refrigerator / Was

4 the walls / color / in the kitchen? / were / What

5 big? / Were / the bedrooms

6 your home / nice? / Was

C ▶ **Now go to page 140. Look at the grammar chart and do the grammar exercise for 11.2.**

4 SPEAKING

A **Draw a picture or plan of a room in your house from your past. Include furniture and your favorite things.**

B PAIR WORK **Work with a partner. Ask and answer questions about your rooms.**

> This is the bedroom. There was a bed, a desk, and two windows.

> What color was the bed?

> My bed was white.

11.3 I HAVE NO IDEA

1 FUNCTIONAL LANGUAGE

A Look at the picture of the woman. Do you know her name? What else do you know about her?

B ◀)) 2.46 Read and listen. What does the man want to remember? Does he remember it?

◀)) 2.46 Audio script

A I'm going to watch *Titanic* tonight.

B The movie?

A Yeah. With Leonardo DiCaprio, and … who was the other actor? The woman?

B Um, **I have no idea.**

A She's from England.

B Sorry, **I'm not sure.**

A Her first name is Kate, **I think.**

B Let me think. **Maybe** it's Kate Hudson? No, she's American. Why don't we look online?

A Good idea. Let's see … *Titanic* actor, woman … Kate Winslet!

B Oh, yeah.

A What was the name of that other movie she was in? With Johnny Depp.

B Oh no … Not again!

GLOSSARY

actor (*n*) a man or woman in a movie, TV show, or play

C Complete the chart with expressions in **bold** from the conversation above.

Expressing uncertainty	
Very unsure	**A little unsure**
I have ¹_____.	Her first name is Kate, I ³_____.
I'm ²_____.	I think her first name is Kate.
I don't know.	⁴_____ it's Kate Hudson?

D ◀)) 2.47 [PAIR WORK] Complete the conversations with the correct words from the box. Listen and check. Then practice with a partner.

> don't   Maybe   no   not   think

1 A When was the movie *Titanic* in theaters?

   B I _____ know. _____ it was in 1997?

2 A How many movies was Kate Winslet in?

   B I have _____ idea.

3 A Where was Melinda yesterday?

   B I _____ she was at home.

4 A Where are the restrooms?

   B Sorry, I'm _____ sure.

2 REAL-WORLD STRATEGY

> **TAKING TIME TO THINK**
>
> When you need time to think about an answer, say, *Let me think, Uh,* or *Um.*
>
> *Um, I have no idea.*
>
> *Let me think. Maybe it's Kate Hudson?*

A   Read the information in the box about taking time to think. Which <u>two</u> expressions does the woman use?

B   🔊 2.48 Listen to a conversation. What is the man sure about? What <u>isn't</u> he sure about?

C   🔊 2.48 Listen again. Which <u>two</u> expressions does the man use when he needs time to think?

D   ▶ PAIR WORK   Student A: Go to page 158. Student B: Go to page 160. Follow the instructions.

3 PRONUNCIATION: Saying /oʊ/ and /ɑː/ vowel sounds

A   🔊 2.49 Listen and repeat the words. How are the vowel sounds different?

/oʊ/   kn**o**w   /ɑː/   n**o**t

B   🔊 2.50 Listen. Write A for words with /oʊ/, for example *know*. Write B for words with /ɑː/, for example *not*.

1   don't ___   3   no ___   5   home ___

2   on ___   4   go ___   6   concert ___

C   🔊 2.51   PAIR WORK   Look at the letters in **bold** below. Listen and repeat. Then practice the conversations with a partner.

1   **A**   Was M**o**na at the c**o**ncert yesterday?   3   **A**   D**o**n't g**o**!

   B   N**o**, she wasn't. She was at h**o**me.   **B**   S**o**rry, I have to g**o** h**o**me.

2   **A**   Where is Leonard**o** DiCapri**o** fr**o**m?   4   **A**   Are we **o**n the right bus? It's very sl**o**w.

   B   I have n**o** idea.   **B**   I d**o**n't know.

4 SPEAKING

GROUP WORK   Think of a movie. Ask other people in your group about the actors in it. Then change roles.

> Who was in the first *Avatar*?

> I have no idea.

> Um, was Zoe Saldana in it?

> Yes, she was.

11.4 THINGS WE KEEP

LESSON OBJECTIVE
- write an email about things you keep from your past

1 READING

A Look at the pictures. What things can you see? Are the things old or new? Do you have some of these things?

B READ FOR MAIN IDEAS Read the article. What is it about?

PICTURING MEMORIES

Terry Lawrence is a travel writer for Pak Airlines in-flight magazine. Today she takes a break from travel writing and tells Pak Airlines readers about what she does in her free time.

I love to travel, I love to write – and I love to take pictures! I often take pictures of people and their favorite things. I have hundreds of pictures of people and the things they keep. People around the world keep things from childhood, for example toy cars, books, and games. These were their first favorite things. And me? I like to keep photographs, of course! Here are some of my favorite pictures.

Meet Tom Bradley and his toy cars. They were birthday gifts. They're old, but he plays with them today – with a little help!

Many parents keep their children's things, like baby shoes or a child's first clothes. Rosa Ortiz keeps her daughter's shoe and her son's shoe in her car. They were one and two years old at the time. Now they're 12 and 13!

Many people keep books and comic books. This is Doug and one of his comic books, but it's not his favorite. Doug leaves his favorite comic book at home – it's very expensive!

GLOSSARY
childhood (*n*) the time when you were a child
keep (*v*) have something for a long time

C READ FOR DETAIL Read again. Then read these sentences from the article. What do the underlined words mean? Circle the answers.

1 <u>These</u> were their first favorite things.

These =   **a** children   **b** birthday gifts   **c** things from their childhood

2 <u>They</u>'re old, but he plays with <u>them</u> today.

They and *them* =   **a** toy cars   **b** shoes   **c** games

3 <u>They</u> were one and two years old at the time.

They =   **a** Rosa's cars   **b** Rosa's parents   **c** Rosa's children

4 <u>It</u>'s not his favorite.

It =   **a** Doug   **b** Doug's comic book   **c** Doug's house

D PAIR WORK What things do you keep? Why? Do you keep the same things from the article, too? Tell a partner.

2 WRITING

A **Read Angie's email to her brother. What things from the past does she find in a box?**

Hi Eddie,

Do you remember this postcard? It was in a box under my bed. It was from Grandpa Bowman in 1969. He was in Saudi Arabia. His postcards were always exciting, and this one was my favorite. The desert is really beautiful. Do *you* have any of his old postcards?

There was also a lot of homework from my school days in the box. Hey, I was smart! Well, usually. My math homework was awful! 🙀 I don't think I want to keep it.

Your old soccer ball was in the box, too. ⚽ Why do I have it? I don't know. There's some writing on it. Maybe it's the autograph of a famous soccer player. Do you want it?

Love,

Angie

GLOSSARY
autograph (*n*) name in handwriting, usually of a famous person

REGISTER CHECK

Use emojis (small pictures) in texts, social media posts, and informal emails. Do **not** use them in formal emails, for example, emails for college or work.

My math homework was awful! 🙀

B | PAIR WORK | | THINK CRITICALLY | Why does Angie's email have three paragraphs?

C | WRITING SKILLS | Read the topic sentence from the email below. The topic sentence tells you what the paragraph is about. Read the email again and <u>underline</u> the three topic sentences.

Do you remember this postcard? (= this paragraph is about a postcard.)

WRITE IT

D Imagine you have a box of old things from your childhood. Write an email to a friend about <u>two</u> or <u>three</u> things in the box. Use a new paragraph for each thing. Write a topic sentence for each paragraph. You can use emojis.

E | PAIR WORK | Read your partner's email. What interesting things do they write about in their email?

TIME TO SPEAK
TV memories

A **PREPARE** Work with a partner. Talk about old TV shows you remember from your childhood. Write notes.

B **AGREE** Compare your ideas with other students. Which shows do a lot of people remember?

C **DISCUSS** Choose a TV show from your conversations in exercise A or B. What do you remember about it? Talk about the names, places, and things in the show.

FIND IT **D** **PREPARE** Prepare a presentation about your TV show from exercise C. Include the ideas below and your own ideas. You can go online and find information you don't remember.

When was it on TV?

What were the places in the show?

TV show

Who were the characters (names, ages, personalities)?

Why was the show popular?

E **PRESENT** Present your memories of the TV show to the class with your partner. Which shows does everyone remember?

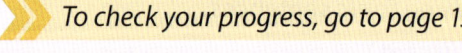

To check your progress, go to page 155.

USEFUL PHRASES

DISCUSS
I remember … from my childhood.
What about you?
Let's talk about the characters in …
What were their names?
I liked that show because …

AGREE
What do you remember?
A lot of people / I remember …

PRESENT
We're talking about …
Our show was really popular.
It was on TV in (year).

UNIT OBJECTIVES

- talk about snacks and small meals
- talk about meals in restaurants
- offer and accept food and drink
- write a restaurant review
- create a menu for a restaurant

STOP, EAT, GO

12

START SPEAKING

A   Which meal do you think these men are eating: breakfast, lunch, or dinner? Is it a big meal or a small meal? Are they enjoying their food?

B   For a good meal, you need good food – and what else? Do you see these things in the picture?

C   Talk about a good meal you remember. You can talk about where and when it was, who you were with, and why it was good.

12.1 BACKPACKING AND SNACKING

LESSON OBJECTIVE
- talk about snacks and small meals

1 VOCABULARY: Snacks and small meals

A 🔊 2.52 PAIR WORK **Listen and repeat. Then choose something you want to eat now.**

| apple | beef | butter | chicken | crackers | orange | potato | soup |

| banana | bread | cheese | coconut | lamb | pineapple | sandwich | tomato |

> **!** To make these words plural, add *-s* or *-es*:
>
> banana → banana**s**   tomato → tomato**es**   sandwich → sandwich**es**
>
> Some nouns are non-count, for example *cheese* and *soup*.

B ▶ **Now do the vocabulary exercises for 12.1 on page 151.**

C PAIR WORK **Look at the pictures in exercise 1A and find:**
- <u>seven</u> words for fruit and vegetables
- <u>three</u> words for meat
- <u>two</u> words for dairy products
- <u>two</u> words for grain products
- <u>two</u> words for small meals

2 LANGUAGE IN CONTEXT

A **Read the blog. Where was Tyler yesterday? Where was he last week?**

B **Read again. Check (✓) the sentences that are true. Correct the false ones.**
- ☐ 1 Tyler's breakfast and lunch were big.
- ☐ 2 There was meat in Tyler's sandwich.
- ☐ 3 There were dairy products in Tyler's breakfast, lunch, and dinner.
- ☐ 4 There are dairy products and fruit in *locro*.

TRAVEL WITH TYLER

Hello from Salvador, Brazil! I'm happy to be here after a really long trip. Yesterday, I took the bus from Aracaju. I didn't eat a lot for breakfast before the trip – just some **bread** and **butter**. Then I was on the bus for seven hours. We stopped in a lot of places, but I stayed on the bus, so I didn't have a big lunch. I ate some **crackers** and a **banana**, and I drank a bottle of warm water (yuck!)

I arrived in Salvador in the afternoon, and I was *really* hungry, so I didn't wait. I had dinner at the bus station! I went to a food stand, and I bought a *bauru* **sandwich**. It's bread with **beef**, **cheese**, and **tomatoes**. I needed it! And I liked it – I'm going to eat it again tomorrow.

South American food is great. Last week, in Quito, Ecuador, I tried *locro*. It's a **soup** with **potatoes** and cheese. I love the fruit in South America, too, but because I'm "backpacking and snacking," it's not always easy to eat. You can't eat **pineapples** and **coconuts** on a bus!

> **GLOSSARY**
> **food stand** (*n*) a place to buy food on the street
> **hungry** (*adj*) you need to eat

3 GRAMMAR: Simple past statements

A (Circle) **the correct answers. Use the sentences in the grammar box to help you.**

1 Use the simple past to talk about **finished events** / **events that are happening now**.

2 After *I*, *you*, *he*, *she*, *we*, *they* and *it*, simple past verbs have **the same** / **different** spelling.

3 Simple past verbs can be regular or irregular. To make most regular past simple verbs, add **-d or -ed** / **-s**.

4 To make negative statements in the simple past, use **don't** / **didn't** + verb (for example, *eat*, *drink*, or *have*).

> ### Simple past statements
>
> Yesterday, I **took** the bus from Aracaju.   I **didn't eat** a lot for breakfast.
>
> I **had** some soup. He **had** a big dinner.   She **didn't like** the sandwich.
>
> She **wanted** an orange. We **wanted** some apples.   They **didn't drink** the coffee.

> **!**   Irregular past simple verbs do not end in *-ed*. For example, *I took the bus*, <u>not</u> *I taked the bus*.
>
>   eat → ate   drink → drank   have → had   go → went   take → took   buy → bought
>
>   For more irregular verbs, see the table at the back of this book.

B **Read the information about irregular verbs in the Notice box. Then** (circle) **the correct words.**

1 It was a really big sandwich, but I *ate* / *eat* it all.

2 We *have* / *had* fish for dinner last night.

3 She didn't *buy* / *bought* food at the supermarket.

4 I was hungry and really *needed* / *need* some food.

5 We *arrive* / *arrived* at the restaurant at 5:30, but it wasn't open.

6 Was the cheese good? I didn't *tried* / *try* it.

C ▶ **Now go to page 140. Look at the grammar charts and do the grammar exercise for 12.1.**

D PAIR WORK **Complete the sentences so they're true for you. Then compare with a partner.**

1 For breakfast, I ate _____ , and I drank _____ .

2 Last week, I bought _____ at the supermarket.

3 The last movie I watched was _____ .

4 Last weekend, I went to _____ with _____ .

4 SPEAKING

A PAIR WORK **Talk about the food in exercise 1A. Say which things you like and which you <u>don't</u> like. For ideas, watch June's video.**

REAL STUDENT

Do you like/not like the same things as June?

B PAIR WORK **Give examples of snacks and small meals you ate last week. Ask your partner questions about what they ate.**

Yesterday, I ate a sandwich for lunch.

Was it good?

WHAT DID YOU EAT?

1 VOCABULARY: Food, drinks, and desserts

A 🔊 **2.53** Look at the pictures. Listen and repeat.

B **PAIR WORK** Which things in exercise 1A are drinks? Which are desserts? Which ones do you like? Which <u>don't</u> you like?

C ▶ Now do the vocabulary exercises for 12.2 on page 151.

D **GROUP WORK** What do you usually eat and drink for breakfast, lunch, and dinner? Tell your group. For ideas, watch Anderson's video.

REAL STUDENT

What's Anderson's food routine? Is your routine the same or different?

rice

steak
black beans
eggs

pizza soda

fish
green beans

ice cream
chocolate cake

juice
water

2 LANGUAGE IN CONTEXT

A 🔊 **2.54** Jackie and Yoo-ri are writing comments on a restaurant review card. Read and listen. Did they like their meal?

B 🔊 **2.54** Read and listen again. What did Jackie and Yoo-ri eat? What did they drink?

🔊 2.54 Audio script

Jackie Look, a comment card. Let's do it.

Yoo-ri OK. We have time before dessert.

Jackie Number one. "What did you eat?" You had **fish** and **rice**. Did you have any vegetables?

Yoo-ri Yeah. I had beans, **black beans**.

Jackie That's right. And I had the **steak** with potatoes and **green beans**. OK. Number 2. "What did you drink?" I just had **water**. Did you have apple **juice**?

Yoo-ri No, I didn't have any juice. I had a **soda**.

Jackie Oh, yeah. OK, number 3. "How was the food?" My steak was great, but I didn't like the potatoes. The green beans were OK. Did you like the fish?

Yoo-ri Yes, I did. It was wonderful, and the rice and beans were good, too. But my soda was warm.

Jackie Hmm … I'm going to check "good." Ah, the server is coming with dessert. Oh, wow! Look at our **chocolate cake** and **ice cream**.

Yoo-ri Yum! Change "good" to "great!"

Clinton Street Restaurant
201 Clinton Street 📞 219–555–2310

Tell us what you think!

Name(s): _Jackie_ and _Yoo-ri_
1 What did you eat? _____
2 What did you drink? _____
3 How was the food?
  ○ great ○ good ○ OK ○ awful
4 Were you happy with your server? ○ yes ○ no
5 How did you hear about us?
  ○ a friend ○ online ○ walking by ○ other

INSIDER ENGLISH

Some people use *waiter* for a man and *waitress* for a woman. But these days, many people use the word *server* for a man or a woman.

3 GRAMMAR: Simple past questions; *any*

A (Circle) the correct answers. Use the information in the grammar box and the Notice box to help you.

1 In simple past *yes/no* questions, use **Did** / **Do** + verb.

2 In simple past information questions, the question word and *did* go **before** / **after** the person or thing.

3 You can use *any* with **yes/no** / **information** questions in the simple past.

Simple past questions	
Yes/no questions	**Information questions**
Did you **have** apple juice?	**How did** you **hear** about us?
Did she **like** the fish?	**What** did they **eat**?
Did they **eat** any ice cream?	

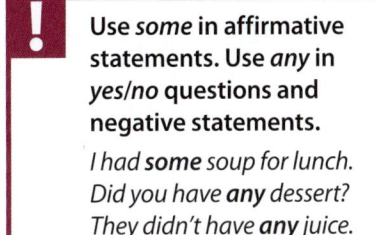

Use *some* in affirmative statements. Use *any* in *yes/no* questions and negative statements.
*I had **some** soup for lunch.*
*Did you have **any** dessert?*
*They didn't have **any** juice.*

B `PAIR WORK` Complete the conversations with the simple past form of the verbs in parentheses ( ). Then practice with a partner and make the answers true for you.

1 **A** _____ you _____ (eat) breakfast?

   B Yes, I _____ .

2 **A** What _____ you _____ (have) for lunch?

   B I _____ an egg sandwich.

3 **A** _____ your friends _____ (go out) for dinner last night?

   B No, they _____ .

4 **A** What _____ your sisters _____ (buy) at the mall?

   B They _____ some shoes. They _____ any lunch.

5 **A** _____ your teacher _____ (give) you any homework?

   B No, she _____ .

C ▶ Now go to page 141. Look at the grammar charts and do the grammar exercise for 12.2.

D `PAIR WORK` Write questions with these words. Use your ideas for the words in parentheses ( ). Then ask and answer the questions with a partner.

what / do / (time or day)	have (food item) / for (meal) / yesterday	where / go / (time or day)

4 SPEAKING

A `PAIR WORK` You're going to ask your partner about a meal they had in a restaurant. Ask the questions from the comment card and the box below. Then think of <u>two</u> more questions.

Where did you eat?	Was the food expensive?
Did you have any dessert?	Was the restaurant busy?
Did you wait for a table?	Who did you eat with?

B `PAIR WORK` Ask and answer the questions from exercise 4A about a meal you ate last week or a favorite meal you had in the past.

> Where did you eat?

> I had dinner at The Fish Dish.

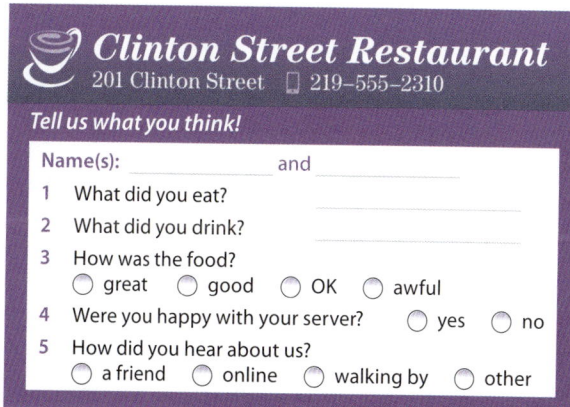

☕ *Clinton Street Restaurant*
201 Clinton Street 📱 219–555–2310

Tell us what you think!

Name(s): _____ and _____

1 What did you eat? _____
2 What did you drink? _____
3 How was the food?
   ○ great ○ good ○ OK ○ awful
4 Were you happy with your server? ○ yes ○ no
5 How did you hear about us?
   ○ a friend ○ online ○ walking by ○ other

12.3 PLEASE PASS THE BUTTER

1 FUNCTIONAL LANGUAGE

A 🔊 **2.55** Elisa has dinner in two different places on different nights. Read and listen to two conversations. What food and drink does Elisa want? What doesn't she want?

> 🔊 **2.55 Audio script**
>
> **1 Elisa** I really like this fish, Dan. It's so good!
>
> **Dan** Thanks. **Do you want** some more?
>
> **Elisa** Yes, please. Thanks. **Can I have** some bread, please?
>
> **Dan** **Of course.** Here. **Would you like** some potatoes?
>
> **Elisa** No, thanks, but **please pass** the butter.
>
> **Dan** OK. **Here you are.**
>
> **2 Server** What would you like to eat?
>
> **Elisa** **I'd like** the chicken and rice, please.
>
> **Server** **All right.** And what would you like to drink?
>
> **Elisa** **Do you have** iced tea?
>
> **Server** Yes. **We have** small and large iced teas.
>
> **Elisa** I'd like a large iced tea, please. It's so hot today!

B Complete the chart with expressions in **bold** from the conversations above. Then read the information in the Accuracy check box. What food does Elisa request with *some*?

GLOSSARY
more (*det*) another piece (of fish, for example)
iced tea (*n*) cold tea

Offering food and drink	Requesting food and drink
1 _____ some more?	4 _____ some bread, please?
2 _____ some potatoes?	5 _____ the butter.
3 _____ to eat? / to drink?	6 _____ the chicken and rice, please.
What would you like for dessert?	7 _____ iced tea?

Responding to requests

Of ⁸ _____ .

Here. / Here ⁹ _____ .

All ¹⁰ _____ . / OK.

¹¹ _____ small and large iced teas.

✔ ACCURACY CHECK

Use *any* in questions.

Did you have any vegetables?

You can use *some* when a question is a request.

Can I have ~~any~~ bread? ✗
Can I have some bread? ✓

C 🔊 **2.56** [PAIR WORK] Put the two conversations in the correct order. Listen and check. Then practice with a partner.

1 ___ Yes, please. It's good!
  ___ OK. Here you are.
  ___ Would you like some more chicken?
  ___ And please pass the potatoes.

2 ___ No, sorry.
  ___ What would you like for dessert?
  ___ I see. OK, I'd like ice cream and coffee, please.
  ___ Let me think. Do you have any chocolate cake?

2 REAL-WORLD STRATEGY

USING *SO* AND *REALLY* TO MAKE WORDS STRONGER

Use *so* before adjectives to make them stronger. Use *really* before some verbs to make them stronger, for example: *like, love, don't like, need (to), want (to), have to.*

Elisa I *really* like this fish, Dan. It's *so* good!

Elisa I'd like a large iced tea. It's *so* hot today!

A **Read the information in the box above about making words stronger. What adjectives does Elisa use with *so*? What verb does she use with *really*?**

B ◀)) **2.57** **Listen to a conversation. What does the man ask for?**

C ◀)) **2.57** **Listen again. What words does he use after *so* and *really*?**

3 PRONUNCIATION: Saying /h/ and /r/ sounds

A ◀)) **2.58** **Listen and repeat the words. Focus on the /h/ and /r/ sounds. How are they different?**

/h/ have   /r/ really

B ◀)) **2.59** **Listen. What sound do you hear? Write /h/ or /r/.**

1	___ear	**3**	___ight	**5**	___appy	**7**	___ad
2	___ave	**4**	___ead	**6**	___ice	**8**	___ed

C ◀)) **2.60** **PAIR WORK** **Listen. Then practice the conversations with a partner. Does your partner say /h/ and /r/ clearly?**

1 A How is your food?
B It's good. I really like this rice.

2 A Where did you go last night?
B We had dinner at The Happy Home restaurant.

3 A How did you hear about us?
B I had an email from a friend. He really likes the food here.

4 SPEAKING

A **PAIR WORK** **Have a conversation. Use exercise 1C for an example. Choose <u>one</u> of these situations:**

- You're at a friend's home. One person offers food. The other person asks for things.
- You're at a restaurant. One person is a server. The other person orders a meal.
- You're at a café. One person is a server. The other person orders a drink and a snack.

Would you like some chicken, Matias?

Yes, please.

B **GROUP WORK** **Have your conversation again, in front of another pair. Listen. What situation in exercise 4A is it? What food and drink do they talk about?**

12.4 WHAT DID THE REVIEWERS SAY?

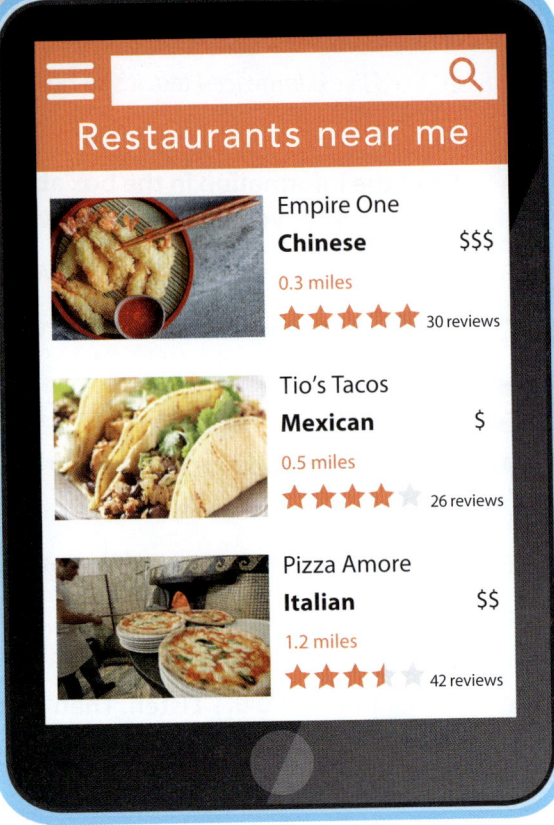

Restaurants near me

Empire One
Chinese $$$
0.3 miles
★★★★★ 30 reviews

Tio's Tacos
Mexican $
0.5 miles
★★★★☆ 26 reviews

Pizza Amore
Italian $$
1.2 miles
★★★⯨☆ 42 reviews

1 LISTENING

A Look at the pictures. What are the people doing? Do you use similar apps?

B ◀)) **2.61** **LISTEN FOR DETAILS** Listen to the conversation. What food does Mara want to eat?

C ◀)) **2.61** **LISTEN FOR SUPPORTING DETAILS** (Circle) the reasons for each statement. Sometimes, there is more than one answer.

1 Eric wants to eat at a restaurant near where they are.

   a He likes to eat in the car.   **b** His favorite restaurants are in the area.   **c** He's hungry.

2 Mara and Eric don't go to Fish Around.

   a Mara doesn't like fish.   **b** Mara ate there in the past.   **c** Eric had a bad meal there.

3 They don't go to Kayla B's Kitchen.

   a The food was bad.   **b** It took a long time to get food.   **c** The restaurant isn't new.

4 They go to Tio's Tacos.

   a It has good reviews.   **b** Mara had a good meal there before.   **c** It's Eric's favorite restaurant.

2 PRONUNCIATION: Listening for *Do you want to ... ?*

A ◀)) **2.62** Listen and repeat. Focus on the <u>underlined</u> words. How is the pronunciation different than the written words?

1 Where <u>do you want to</u> eat?   **2** <u>Do you want</u> Chinese, Mexican, or Italian food?

B ◀)) **2.63** Listen to three speakers. How do they say *want to*? Match the speaker (1–3) with the pronunciation (a–c).

  a wanna ___   **b** /dʒu/ want ___   **c** /dʒu/ wanna ___

A **Read two reviews of the restaurant Fish Around. What did Frank and Julieta eat? What was their favorite thing?**

Fish Around
Los Angeles, United States

$$ Fish   ★★★★☆ 98 reviews

Frank B. ★★★★☆

Los Angeles, USA This is a nice restaurant. It's big, and it has a lot of windows, so it's very light. There are some tall plants in the dining area, but it isn't a "forest." I had vegetable soup, fish, and rice. The soup was good. I love fish, and the fish was great! My brother had fish and vegetables, and he liked his meal, too. We both had dessert. He had cake and I had ice cream. The servers were so friendly. We were really happy with our meal, and it wasn't expensive.

Julieta F. ★★★☆☆

Buenos Aires, Argentina I think this is a good restaurant, but I didn't choose it. My friends like fish, so they wanted to eat here. I like meat, but there wasn't any meat on the menu. Was the food good? Well, my friends liked it. They had fish, vegetables, rice, and dessert. I had fish and potatoes. The potatoes were OK. The fish was … well, it was fish! For dessert, I had pineapple cake and coconut ice cream. Wow! It was so good! I'm giving this restaurant three stars because the dessert was so great. The servers were nice. The price was OK – not cheap, but not expensive.

B **PAIR WORK** **THINK CRITICALLY** **Did Frank and Julieta like their meals? Why or why not?**

C **Read the sentences from the reviews. Underline the things the people ate.**

My brother had fish and vegetables.

I had vegetable soup, fish, and rice.

D **WRITING SKILLS** **Read the rules about writing lists, below. Circle the correct answers. Use the sentences in exercise 3C to help you. Then underline all the lists of food in the reviews.**

1 To list two things, you can join them with *and*. **Do / don't** use a comma (,) between two things.

2 To list three or more things, you can use a comma (,) between the things. Use *and* **before / after** the last thing.

> **REGISTER** CHECK
>
> In informal writing, you can sometimes ask and answer your own questions.
>
> *Was the food good? Well, my friends liked it.*

🖊️ **WRITE IT**

E **Write a review of a restaurant you like. You can write about:**
  - the restaurant's appearance
  - the food you ate
  - your opinion about the food
  - your opinion about the servers
  - the price of the food

F **GROUP WORK** **Read other people's reviews. Would you like to eat at any of the restaurants?**

TIME TO SPEAK
Recipe for a great restaurant

A   **DISCUSS**   Talk about a great restaurant you went to, and say why you liked it. Then talk about a bad restaurant, and say why you <u>didn't</u> like it.

B   **PREPARE**   Talk about what makes a great restaurant. Think about the things you discussed in exercise A and the things below. Then compare your ideas with other people.

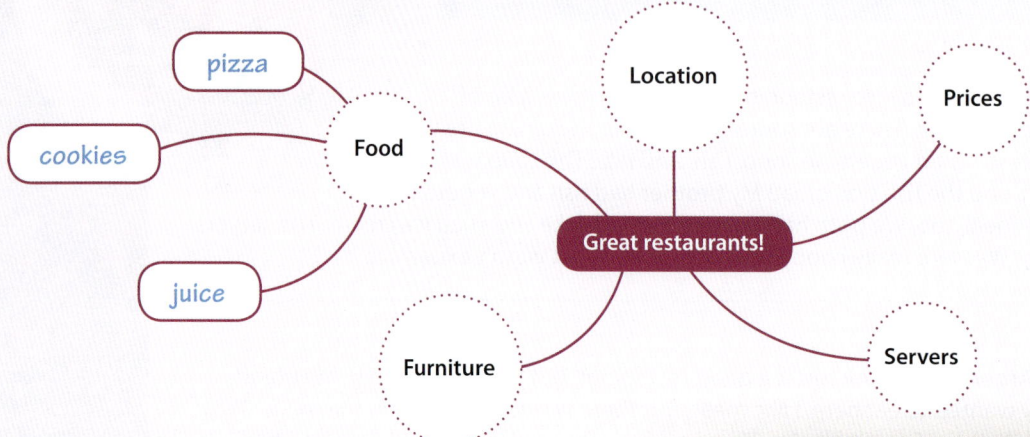

FIND IT

C   **DECIDE**   Work with a partner. Imagine you're opening a new restaurant. Choose a name for your restaurant and talk about the food and drink it has. Then create a great menu. You can go online to find ideas.

D   **ROLE PLAY**   Work with another pair. Welcome them to your restaurant. They choose a meal from your menu. Then change roles. Continue with other pairs.

E   **PRESENT**   Tell the class about some of the menus in exercise D. Were they good? What did you choose? What's your favorite menu?

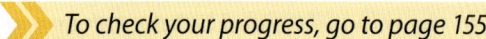
To check your progress, go to page 155.

USEFUL PHRASES

DECIDE
OK. First, what's the name of our restaurant?
What kind of food do we have?
Let's plan a great menu. We can have …

ROLE PLAY
Welcome to our restaurant!
What would you like to eat/drink?
Do you have … ?
So, you would like …

PRESENT
We went to a great restaurant. Its name was …
We liked / didn't like …
Our favorite menu is … because …

REVIEW 4 (UNITS 10–12)

1 VOCABULARY

A **Look at the groups of words (1–6). For each group, ⟨circle⟩ the word that does not belong. Then match the groups with the categories (a–d). Some groups match the same category.**

1	cheese	fish	potato	chicken	coat	___	
2	white	winter	rainy season	summer	dry season	___	**a** colors
3	red	green	brown	fall	yellow	___	**b** clothes
4	shirt	dress	skirt	pants	rice	___	**c** food
5	purple	blue	shorts	gray	black	___	**d** seasons
6	banana	tomato	apple	pink	cake	___	

B **Match each word you ⟨circled⟩ in 1–6 to a different category (a–d). Then add <u>one</u> extra word to the categories.**

2 GRAMMAR

A **Make questions and answers in the simple past. Use the words in parentheses ( ).**

1 **A** _____ you _____ a good weekend? (have)

   B Yes, it _____ great, thanks. (be)

2 **A** What _____ you _____ ? (eat)

   B We _____ some Japanese food. (try)

3 **A** Where _____ you on Saturday? (be)

   B I _____ at home in the morning, but not in the afternoon. (be)

4 **A** What _____ you _____ on TV last night? (watch)

   B A movie, but it _____ very good. (not be)

5 **A** _____ you _____ to the supermarket? (go)

   B Yes, but we _____ a lot. (not buy)

6 **A** _____ you busy yesterday? (be)

   B Yes, I _____ all day. (work)

B **PAIR WORK** **Talk to a partner. Ask and answer <u>five</u> questions about things you did this month. Use the questions above, or your own ideas.**

C **Complete the paragraph. Use simple past forms of the verbs in parentheses ( ).**

At the airport, I ¹ _____ (go) to a store, and I ² _____ (buy) a cup of coffee and a sandwich. I ³ _____ (drink) the coffee, but I didn't have time to eat the sandwich. So I ⁴ _____ (take) it on the plane, and I ⁵ _____ (eat) it on the flight. I ⁶ _____ (have) lunch over the Atlantic Ocean. It was cool!

D **Write about a meal you had this month. Say when and where you had it, and what you ate.**

3 SPEAKING

A **PAIR WORK** **Talk about a day out or trip you went on.**

> On Saturday, I went out with some friends. We took a walk.

> Where did you go?

B **Write <u>three</u> sentences about your day out or trip. Compare with a partner. Were your days the same or different?**

4 FUNCTIONAL LANGUAGE

A Complete the conversation with the words in the box.

can't	don't	have	idea	Let	Let's	maybe	sorry	sure	think

Min-jun Why ¹_____ we go out on Friday night?

Jamie Um … I'm ²_____, but I ³_____. I ⁴_____ to help my father on Friday.

Min-jun What about Saturday night?

Jamie ⁵_____ me think. Yes, sure. Saturday's fine.

Min-jun OK. ⁶_____ meet at Calendar Café. Do you know it?

Jamie I'm not ⁷_____. Is it on Fourth Avenue?

Min-jun Yes. Near the movie theater.

Jamie OK, great. What time?

Min-jun The café is busy on Saturday night, I ⁸_____. Let's get there early. How about 6 o'clock?

Jamie Good ⁹_____. Then ¹⁰_____ we can go to a movie after dinner.

B Read the conversation and (circle) the correct words.

Yuri I ¹ *really / so* like this lamb.

Susan Thanks. Would you ² *want / like* some more?

Yuri ³ *Yes, / No,* please. ⁴ *Can / Would* I have some more green beans, too?

Susan ⁵ *A / Of* course. ⁶ *Here / Have* you are. Oh, please ⁷ *pass / give* the potatoes, Yuri.

Yuri All ⁸ *course / right*. Here.

5 SPEAKING

A [PAIR WORK] Choose **one** of the situations below. Talk to a partner. Have a conversation.

1 You and your friend want to go out this weekend. Make suggestions about what you can do and where / what time you can meet. Look at page 102 for useful language.

> Let's go out on Saturday night.

2 A friend asks you about a movie. He/She wants to know the names of the actors in the movie, their nationalities, and other movies they are in. You are not 100% sure. Look at page 112 for useful language.

> Who was in *The Matrix*?

> The first Matrix movie? I'm not sure. He's American, I think. Um …

3 A friend is at your home for dinner. Offer him/her things to eat and drink. Look at page 122 for useful language.

> Would you like some chicken?

B [PAIR WORK] Change roles and have another conversation.

GRAMMAR REFERENCE AND PRACTICE

7.1 PRESENT CONTINUOUS STATEMENTS (page 67)

Present continuous statements		
	Affirmative	**Negative**
I	**'m cooking** breakfast right now.	**'m not cooking** breakfast right now.
He / She / It	**'s helping** the children. **'s taking** a shower. **'s drinking** milk.	**'s not helping** the children. **'s not taking** a shower. **'s not drinking** milk. (the cat)
You / We / They	**'re eating** breakfast. **'re cleaning** the kitchen. **'re learning** a lot at school.	**'re not eating** breakfast. **'re not cleaning** the kitchen. **'re not learning** a lot at school.

A **Put the words in the correct order to make sentences.**

1 My / aren't / TV. / parents / watching
2 coffee. / cup / drinking / a / I'm / of
3 a / She's / now. / bath / taking / right
4 TV / in / room. / Jack / his / watching / is
5 eating / the moment. / They're / breakfast / at
6 isn't / homework. / her / Maria / doing
7 our / helping / We're / now. / grandparents

7.2 PRESENT CONTINUOUS QUESTIONS (page 69)

Present continuous: *yes/no* questions and short answers		
I	**Am** I **talking** to John?	Yes, you **are**. / No, you **'re not**.
He / She / It	**Is** she **cleaning** the house? **Is** he **riding** his bike right now? **Is** it **working** at the moment?	Yes, she **is**. / No, she **'s not**. Yes, he **is**. / No, he **'s not**. Yes, it **is**. / No, it **'s not**.
You / They	**Are** you and your sister **sending** text messages? **Are** they **waiting** at the bus stop?	Yes, we **are**. / No, we **'re not**. Yes, they **are**. / No, they **'re not**.

Present continuous: information questions				
I	**Who**	**am**	I	**talking** to?
He / She / It	**Why** **Where** **How**	**is** **is** **is**	he / she he / she it	**carrying** a bag? **working** today? **going**?
You / We / They	**What** **Who**	**are** **are**	we / you / they	**doing** right now? **waiting** for?

  You can answer *Why* questions with *because*.

Why is he carrying a bag?
*He's carrying a bag **because** he has a lot of books.* (= a complete sentence)
***Because** he has a lot of books.* (= an incomplete sentence in informal speech)

A   **Write questions for the answers. Use the words in parentheses ( ).**

1   A _____ (you / send / a text to Carol)
    B No, I'm not. I'm calling her.

2   A _____ (why / we / wait / for Paul)
    B Because he's driving us home.

3   A _____ (Denny and Pam / do / the dishes)
    B Yes, they are.

4   A _____ (Sandra / wash / the dog)
    B No, she isn't. She's watching TV.

5   A _____ (who / your sister / help / right now)
    B My brother.

8.1   *CAN* AND *CAN'T* FOR ABILITY; *WELL* (page 77)

can and *can't* for ability; *well*				
	Affirmative	**Negative**	**Questions**	**Short answers**
I	**can** paint.	**can't** paint well.	**Can** I dance?	Yes, I **can** No, I **can't**.
He / She / It	**can** paint.	**can't** paint.	**Can** she dance well?	Yes, she **can**. No, she **can't**.
You / We / They	**can** paint well.	**can't** paint.	**Can** they dance?	Yes, they **can**. No, they **can't**.

A   **Put the words in order to make sentences.**

1   can / well. / swim / Cathy   _____

2   a / you / car? / drive / Can   _____

3   play / I / guitar. / can't / the   _____

4   and paint? / you / Can / draw   _____

5   well. / can't / I / very / skateboard   _____

6   fix / My / table. / brother / your / can   _____

7   surf / can't / or snowboard. / I   _____

8   well. / son / can / Their / sing   _____

8.2 *CAN* AND *CAN'T* FOR POSSIBILITY (page 79)

can and *can't* for possibility		
Information questions with *can*		
I	**What can** I eat?	**How can** I pay for the food?
He / She /It	**Where can** he eat?	**How can** he get to the restaurant?
You / We / They	**When can** we eat?	**Who can** we have lunch with today?

A **Read the answers. Then write questions.**

1 A *Where can we work?*
   B We can work <u>in the meeting room</u>.

2 A _____ ?
   B We can watch <u>a movie</u>.

3 A _____ ?
   B We can get to the mall <u>by bus</u>.

4 A _____ ?
   B We can have a meeting <u>on Friday</u>.

5 A _____ ?
   B We can call <u>my cousin</u>.

6 A _____ ?
   B We can <u>play basketball</u>.

7 A _____ ?
   B We can <u>meet at the hotel</u>.

8 A _____ ?
   B We can take a picture <u>with my phone</u>.

9.1 *THIS* AND *THESE* (page 87)

This and *these*	
This is my ticket.	**These** are new boats.
This hotel is cheap.	**These** birds are funny.
Ryan loves **this** farm.	I don't like **these** pictures.

A **Put the words in order to make sentences.**

1 a / is / tour / This / boring.

2 these / I / birds. / like

3 sisters. / are / These / my

4 video. / watching / I'm / this

5 really / animals are / funny. / These

6 isn't / expensive. / This / vacation

9.2 *LIKE TO, WANT TO, NEED TO, HAVE TO* (page 89)

like to, want to		*need to, have to*	
I	**like to play** soccer. **want to play** soccer.	I	**need to work** on Saturday. **have to work** on Saturday.
He / She / It	**likes to play** soccer. **wants to play** soccer.	He / She / It	**needs to work** on Saturday **has to work** on Saturday.
You / We / They	**want to play** soccer. **like to play** soccer.	You / We / They	**need to work** on Saturday. **have to work** on Saturday.

A Complete the sentences with *like to, want to,* or *have to/need to* and the verbs in parentheses ( ).

> **!** You can use *need to* + a verb OR *have to* + a verb to talk about things that are necessary.

1 I _____ (swim) in the ocean, but only in July and August.

2 One day, I _____ (go) to Japan on vacation.

3 My son can't do his homework. I _____ (help) him.

4 I'm late for work, so I _____ (leave) now.

5 This is a great song. I _____ (buy) it.

6 In Japan, you _____ (drive) on the left side of the road.

7 At a movie theater, you _____ (pay) before you watch the movie.

10.1 STATEMENTS WITH *BE GOING TO* (page 99)

Statements with *be going to*		
	Affirmative	**Negative**
I	**'m going to be** home tomorrow.	**'m not going to be** home tomorrow.
He / She / It	**'s going to take** a walk in the park. **'s going to be** warm tomorrow.	**'s not going to go** shopping next week. **isn't going to be** warm tomorrow.
You / We / They	**'re going to be** here next weekend.	**'re not going to be** here next weekend.
Future time expressions		
this evening, tonight, tomorrow	on/next/this Monday	
this week/weekend/month/year	next week/weekend/month/year	

A Write sentences with the correct form of *be going to.*

1 We / not play / soccer this weekend
   We're not going to play soccer this weekend .

2 Vicky / meet / her friends tomorrow
   _____ .

3 You / have / a party for your birthday
   _____ .

4 They / not go / surf / next Saturday
   _____ .

5 I / go / dancing this evening
   _____ .

6 He / not do / the dishes after dinner
   _____ .

10.2 QUESTIONS WITH *BE GOING TO* (page 101)

be going to: yes/no questions		
	yes/no questions	Short answers
I	**Am I going to meet** him at 4:00?	Yes, you **are.** No, you**'re not.**
He / She / It	**Is she going to see** a friend?	Yes, she **is.** No, she**'s not.**
You / We / They	**Are** you **going to take** a hat?	Yes, I **am.** / Yes, we **are.** No, I**'m not.** / No, we**'re not.**

be going to: information questions
When are you **going to leave?**
Where is Sofia **going to go?**
What are we **going to do** today?
What time is he **going to have** lunch?
Who are they **going to meet?**
How are you **going to get** to the airport?

A (Circle) the correct words to complete the sentences.

1 Are you going *buying / to buy* some new jeans?

2 Who is he going to *go / going* shopping with?

3 Is she going to *cook / cooks* dinner for four people tonight?

4 *What / What time* are we going to drive to the airport?

5 Are *your parents / Mariana* going to send him an email?

6 What *they are / are they* going to wear to the party?

11.1 STATEMENTS WITH *WAS* AND *WERE* (page 109)

Statements with *was* and *were*		
	Affirmative	**Negative**
I / He / She / It	**was** in the house.	**wasn't** noisy.
You / We / They	**were** at work.	**weren't** there.

A Complete the posts with the affirmative or negative form of *was* or *were.*

Carlene Rauss I remember a great vacation. It ¹_____ January 2010, and we ²_____ in Argentina. It ³_____ summer, so the weather ⁴_____ great! Buenos Aires is an exciting city, so we ⁵_____ really happy there. #flashbackfriday #2010 #vacation

Paulo Soto I remember my twentieth birthday. My friends and I ⁶_____ at the beach, but the weather ⁷_____ awful! It ⁸_____ really rainy. The café on the beach ⁹_____ open, so there was no food. It's not a good memory because we ¹⁰_____ very happy. I mean, it ¹¹_____ a happy birthday. ☹

👍 9   ❤ 4

11.2 QUESTIONS WITH *WAS* AND *WERE* (page 111)

Questions with *was* and *were*		
	yes/no questions	Short answers
I / He / She	**Was** she at home on Saturday?	Yes, she **was**. / No, she **wasn't**.
You / We / They	**Were** you at home on Saturday?	Yes, I **was**. / No, I **wasn't**.
Information questions with *was* and *were*		
I / He / She	**Where was** he?	
You / We / They	**How old were** you in this photo?	

A   Write questions in the simple past to match the answers.

1 _____ ?   The walls in my bedroom were blue.
2 _____ ?   My last vacation was in Brazil.
3 _____ ?   My brother's birthday party was on Friday.
4 _____ ?   Yes, my parents were at the party.
5 _____ ?   No, my house was small.
6 _____ ?   I was at work on Saturday because I was really busy.

12.1 SIMPLE PAST STATEMENTS (page 119)

Simple past statements
Use the simple past to talk about events that are in the past and finished.
I **ate** a big lunch yesterday.   We **played** soccer last weekend.   We **went** to La Paz last year.
Simple past verbs can be regular or irregular. Simple past regular verbs end in *-ed*.

Some regular verbs				
	-ed	*-d*	double consonant + *ed*	change *-y* to *-ied*
I / You / He / She / We / They	work**ed** play**ed** watch**ed** want**ed** walk**ed**	like**d** love**d** arrive**d** use**d** dance**d**	stop → stop**ped** chat → chat**ted**	try → tr**ied** carry → carr**ied** study → stud**ied**

Some irregular verbs					
Base form	Simple past	Base form	Simple past	Base form	Simple past
have	had	write	wrote	ride	rode
go	went	send	sent	fly	flew
eat	ate	buy	bought	get up	got up
drink	drank	think	thought	leave	left
do	did	run	ran	meet	met
take	took	swim	swam	sing	sang
read	read	drive	drove		

A Complete the chart with the words in the box.

~~arrive~~   buy   drink   eat   go   have
like   need   stay   stop   take   try

Base form	Rule	Simple past
arrive	Add -d.	arrived
	Add -ed.	
	Double p and add -ed.	
	Change -y to -ied.	

Base form	Irregular simple past form

12.2 SIMPLE PAST QUESTIONS; *ANY* (page 121)

Simple past questions		
yes/no questions	**Short answers**	
Did you **have** apple juice?	Yes, I/we **did.**	No, I/we **didn't.**
Did we **arrive** on time?	Yes, we/you **did.**	No, we/you **didn't**
Did she/he **like** the fish?	Yes, she/he **did.**	No, she/he **didn't.**
Did they **go out** for dinner?	Yes, they **did.**	No, they **didn't.**

Information questions		
How did	I / you	**hear** about the restaurant?
What did	you / he / she	**have** for dinner last night?
Who did	we / they	**see** at the party?

any
You can use *any* in *yes/no* questions and negative statements. *Any* = one, some, or all of something. *Not + any* = none.
Use *some* in affirmative statements. You can use *any* and *some* with count and non-count nouns.

Simple past questions and statements with *any*	
yes/no questions	**Negative statements**
Did you have **any** vegetables?	I didn't have **any** juice.
Did Mary buy **any** milk?	Joel didn't eat **any** eggs.
Did they have **any** dessert?	We didn't drink **any** soda.

A Put the words in the correct order to make sentences.

1 for dinner? / chicken / Did / make / you _____

2 they / did / for lunch? / have / What _____

3 eat / Did / any / vegetables? / Tonya _____

4 last night? / Where / she / go / did _____

5 coffee / buy / We / at the store. / didn't / any _____

6 at Pete's Pizza / last year? / you / Did / work _____

VOCABULARY PRACTICE

7.1 ACTIVITIES AROUND THE HOUSE (page 66)

A Match 1–6 with a–f to complete the sentences.

1	Do they cook ____		**a**	her daughter's hair.
2	Karen usually washes ____		**b**	your room on the weekend?
3	I do a lot of ____		**c**	breakfast every morning?
4	They're nice. They help ____		**d**	me with my English.
5	He takes ____		**e**	homework every day.
6	Do you clean ____		**f**	a shower in the evening.

B Add the words in parentheses ( ) to the correct place in each sentence. Then write the sentences.

1 Do you the dishes after lunch? (do)   *Do you do the dishes after lunch?*

2 Rudy his car on the weekend. (drives)

3 Does he his teeth every day? (brush)

4 My mother usually cooks at 6:30. (dinner)

5 She takes a every evening. (bath)

6 I often my grandmother. (help)

7.2 TRANSPORTATION (page 68)

A Complete the sentences with the correct verbs in the box.

driving	going	riding	taking	waiting	walking

1 I'm not _____ to work because my son has my car today.

2 Where are you? Mike is _____ for you at the train station.

3 Carolina is _____ with her dog in the park right now.

4 We're _____ to the mall because we need new shoes.

5 Tonya is _____ her bike to the store.

6 Mark isn't _____ the bus to class because it's late.

B Circle the correct words to complete the sentences.

1 Vic is at *the bus stop / his bike.*

2 Why are you carrying *a plant / the train*?

3 I usually take *the train station / the subway* to work.

4 When are you going to your *parents' house / mall*?

5 I'm sorry. I'm busy. I'm on *the bus stop / the train.*

8.1 VERBS TO DESCRIBE SKILLS (page 76)

A **Complete the sentences with the verbs in the box. You won't use all the verbs.**

dance	fix	play	skateboard	speak
draw	paint	sing	snowboard	swim

1 I don't _____. There's a mountain near me but it doesn't have snow on it.

2 My friends usually _____ the guitar and _____ songs after dinner.

3 In my art class, we _____ and _____ a lot of different things.

4 I _____ two languages – English and Korean.

5 In February and March, I _____ in the ocean.

6 Do you have a problem with your laptop? My brothers _____ computers.

B **Complete the words with vowels (*a, e, i, o, u*).**

1 d _a_ nc _e_

2 f __ x th __ ngs

3 sn __ wb _____ rd

4 sw __ m

5 pl __ y the g _____ t __ r

6 sp _____ k tw __ l __ ng _____ g __ s

7 r _____ d m __ s __ c

8 dr __ w

9 sk __ t __ b _____ rd

10 p _____ nt

11 s __ ng

12 s __ rf

147

8.2 WORK (page 78)

A **Complete the sentences with the words in the box.**

break	coworkers	have	think
company	hard	office	worker

1 I work for a big American _____.
2 I have a new desk and a chair in my _____.
3 She's doing a great job. She's a very good _____.
4 It's time to take a _____ and have a cup of coffee.
5 I work in a team with six _____.
6 We're always busy. We work _____.
7 Can we talk about this? Can we _____ a meeting?
8 I don't know the answer. Can I _____ about it for five minutes?

B (Circle) **the word that doesn't belong in each group.**

1 living room   office   kitchen   bedroom
2 have a meeting   play games   call a coworker   work hard
3 drink coffee   have lunch   take a break   have a meeting
4 company   couch   chair   desk
5 worker   brother   teacher   coworker

9.1 TRAVEL (page 86)

A (Circle) **the correct words to complete the sentences.**

1 I have a *ticket / tour* for the bus.
2 This *city / ranch* is in the country.
3 I'm on *vacation / country* with my family.
4 My seat on the *plane / ticket* is by the window.
5 My house is in a small *town / boat*, but I work in the city.
6 This *tour / ticket* is expensive, but it's really interesting.

B (Circle) **the word that doesn't belong in each group.**

1 vacation   tour   work
2 ranch   farm   ticket   country
3 boat   hotel   plane   bus
4 ticket   tour   plane   friend
5 country   town   city

9.2 TRAVEL ARRANGEMENTS (page 88)

A **Match 1–6 with a–f to complete the sentences.**

1 You can buy tickets ____   a destination.
2 We can check in for our ____   b airport.
3 I don't usually travel on ____   c online.
4 We're arriving at our ____   d trains.
5 I'm staying at a really nice ____   e flight.
6 We're flying from the new ____   f hotel.

B **David is traveling from Chicago to London. Put his trip in the correct order.**

_g_ → ____ → ____ → ____ → ____ → ____ → ____ → ____

a Stay in the hotel.
b Drive to the airport.
c Arrive at the hotel.
d Leave home.
e Take a bus from the airport to the hotel.
f Check in for the flight at the airport.
g Buy a plane ticket online.
h Fly to the destination.

10.1 GOING OUT (page 98)

A **Circle the correct word to complete the sentences.**

1 Can you *meet* / *go* me at the airport on Friday?
2 Jennifer wants to *take* / *look* her brother to lunch for his birthday.
3 We're *doing* / *having* a picnic right now.
4 I like to *get* / *meet* together with friends on the weekends.
5 Do you usually *make* / *go* shopping at the mall?
6 I never *take* / *eat* outside.

B **Complete the sentences with the words in the box.**

> art   coffee   family   hotel   shopping   walk

1 Do you want to take a _____ in the park?
2 I like to look at interesting _____ in museums.
3 I want to take you out for _____ to my favorite café.
4 We often get together with _____ on the weekends.
5 I have to meet my coworker at his _____ on Friday.
6 Maria never goes _____ with us. She doesn't like it.

10.2 CLOTHES; SEASONS (page 100)

A **Complete the clothes words with vowels (*a, e, i, o, u*).**

1 I want to buy some j____ns and a sw____t____r.
2 I'm going to wear a T-sh____rt and sh____rts to the beach.
3 This store sells sh____s and b____ts.
4 I'm going to buy a winter c____t and h____t.
5 We usually wear p____nts and a sh____rt at work.
6 Is she going to wear a dr____ss or a sk____rt?

B **Complete the paragraph with the words in the box.**

dry season	fall	rainy season	spring	summer	winter

In Japan, we have four seasons. I love [1]_____ and [2]_____ because there are a lot of flowers then. After summer, it's [3]_____, and this is usually from September to November. Then it's [4]_____, and you can do a lot of fun activities, for example, snowboard in the mountains. We have a short [5]_____, too. It usually starts in June and ends in July, and it is *very* rainy. We don't have a [6]_____ in Japan. It's not a desert country.

11.1 DESCRIBING PEOPLE, PLACES, AND THINGS (page 108)

A **Match the sentences with the correct responses.**

1 This new restaurant isn't good. ____
2 Your daughter is quiet. ____
3 This is a beautiful picture. ____
4 I love beach parties. ____
5 The train was very slow today. ____
6 These children are really noisy. ____

a Thanks. I think the artist is wonderful.
b Really? It's usually fast.
c Yes, but they're really cute.
d That's true. She's really shy.
e I know. The food is awful.
f Me, too. They're exciting, and the ocean is beautiful.

B **Read the sentences and complete the words.**

1 My cousin is **b**_____, and her children are really **c**_____.
2 It's a nice, **q**_____ restaurant, and it has **w**_____ food!
3 This movie is **a**_____. It's **s**_____ and boring.
4 I love soccer games. They're always **n**_____ and **e**_____.
5 My brother's happy because he has a **n**_____ car. It's really **f**_____.

11.2 COLORS (page 110)

A **Unscramble the color words (1–10.) Then match the words to the colors (a–j).**

1 dre _____   a ● ____
2 nreeg _____   b ● ____
3 leub _____   c ● ____
4 tiwhe _____   d ● ____
5 weyoll _____   e ● ____
6 nbwor _____   f ● ____
7 knip _____   g ● ____
8 ragnoe _____   h ● ____
9 ygre _____   i ○ ____
10 klacb _____   j ● ____

B **Match five of the colors in exercise A to the things below.**

1 some milk _____
2 a coffee with milk _____
3 some grass _____
4 the ocean _____
5 an elephant _____

12.1 SNACKS AND SMALL MEALS (page 118)

A **Look at the pictures. Write the words in the chart.**

Fruit and vegetables	Meat	Dairy products	Grains	Small meals

B (Circle) **the correct words to complete the sentences.**

1 **A** What do you want with your crackers?

  B I want cheese and *tomatoes / coconut*, please.

2 For a small meal, I like soup and *bread / potato*.

3 My favorite sandwich has bread, *butter / orange*, and chicken.

4 Beef is very good with *bananas / tomatoes*.

5 My brother really likes fruit. He eats bananas and *apples / lamb* every day.

12.2 MORE FOOD, DRINKS, AND DESSERTS (page 120)

A **Complete the menu with the words in the box.**

| beans | chocolate cake | cookies | ice cream |
| juice | pizza | | soda |

B (Circle) **the correct words to complete the sentences.**

1 *Steak / Rice* is my favorite meat.

2 *Cookies / Green beans* are good for you because they are vegetables.

3 Do you want some *pizza / ice cream* for dessert?

4 I like to eat *eggs / water* for breakfast.

5 Did you drink any *rice / juice* with your meal?

6 *Chocolate cake / soda* is my favorite dessert.

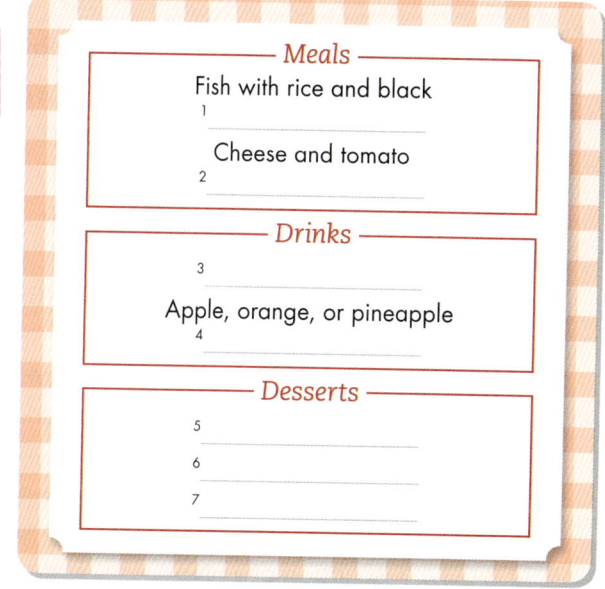

Meals
Fish with rice and black
1
Cheese and tomato
2

Drinks
3
Apple, orange, or pineapple
4

Desserts
5
6
7

PROGRESS CHECK

Can you do these things? Check (✓) what you can do. Then write your answers in your notebook.

UNIT 7	Now I can …	Prove it
	☐ use words about activities around the house.	Write three things you do around the house.
	☐ use the present continuous.	Write a sentence about what you are doing right now. Write a sentence about what your teacher is doing.
	☐ use transportation words.	Complete the sentences with transportation words. *I'm on the _____ right now. Are you _____ to work? We're riding our _____ to the park.*
	☐ ask *yes/no* and information questions in the present continuous.	Write one *yes/no* question and two information questions. Use the present continuous.
	☐ start a phone call.	Write a way to answer the phone. Write a question to ask people how they are.
	☐ write a blog about things happening now.	Read your blog from lesson 7.4. Find a way to improve it. Use the Accuracy check, Register check, and the new language from this unit.

UNIT 8	Now I can …	Prove it
	☐ talk about skills.	Write five skills that your friends or people in your family have. Use *can*.
	☐ use *can* to talk about ability.	Write a sentence about something you can do well and a sentence about something you can't do well.
	☐ talk about work.	Write three things that people do at work.
	☐ use *can* to talk about possibility.	Write two questions. Use *What … ?* and *Where … ? + can*.
	☐ give opinions.	Do you think technology is good for the world? Write a short answer.
	☐ write an online comment.	Read your online comment from lesson 8.4. Find a way to improve it. Use the Accuracy check, Register check, and the new language from this unit.

UNIT 9	Now I can …	Prove it
	☐ use travel words.	Where can you take a tour? What do you need a ticket for? Answer the questions about your city or country.
	☐ use *this* and *these*.	Complete these sentences with your own ideas. *I _____ this _____ . I _____ these _____ .*
	☐ talk about travel arrangements.	Think of a city in your country, or in another country. Describe the trip from your home to the city.
	☐ use *like to, want to, have to, need to.*	Write four sentences about things you like to do, want to do, have to do, and need to do.
	☐ ask for information in a store.	Write three questions to ask for missing information. Begin your questions with *Where … ?, How much … ?,* and *What time does … ?* Then write the answers to your questions.
	☐ write a description of a place.	Read your description of a place from lesson 9.4. Find a way to improve it. Use the Accuracy check, Register check, and the new language from this unit.

154

PROGRESS CHECK

Can you do these things? Check (✓) what you can do. Then write your answers in your notebook.

Now I can …	Prove it
☐ use words for going out activities.	How many going out activities can you remember? Make a list.
☐ use *be going to* in statements.	Write two sentences about what you're going to do next month. Write two sentences about what you're <u>not</u> going to do next year.
☐ use words for clothes and seasons.	What's your favorite season? What do you usually wear to class? What do you wear when you go out with your friends?
☐ ask *yes/no* and information questions with *be going to*.	Complete these questions. Then write answers for you. *Are _____ (you, work) this summer? What _____ (you, do) for your next birthday?*
☐ make and respond to suggestions.	Complete the suggestions with *Why don't we* or *Let's*. Then write answers to the suggestions. *_____ meet at a café tomorrow.* *_____ go shopping after class?*
☐ write an online invitation.	Read your online invitation from lesson 10.4. Find a way to improve it. Use the Accuracy check, Register check, and the new language from this unit.

Now I can …	Prove it
☐ use adjectives to describe people, places, and things.	Write three sentences. Use adjectives to describe a person, a place, and a thing.
☐ use *was* and *were* in statements.	Write four sentences about the past. Use *was*, *were*, *wasn't*, and *weren't*.
☐ talk about colors.	Look around you. What things can you see? What color are they? Write five sentences.
☐ ask questions with *was* and *were*.	Write two questions with *was* and two questions with *were*.
☐ express uncertainty.	Write the capital city of these countries: Australia, Germany, India, Indonesia. In your answer, write that you're not sure.
☐ write an email about things you keep from the past.	Read your email from lesson 11.4. Find a way to improve it. Use the Accuracy check, Register check, and the new language from this unit.

Now I can …	Prove it
☐ talk about snacks and small meals.	Write about food you like and don't like. Write about five things.
☐ use simple past statements.	Write four sentences about things you did yesterday.
☐ talk about food, drinks, and desserts.	Write something you ate yesterday, or last week, for dessert. Write something you drank.
☐ use simple past questions.	Write three questions to ask a partner about what he or she did last week.
☐ offer and request food and drink.	Imagine you're in a restaurant. Write a question the server asks, and write your answer.
☐ write a restaurant review.	Read your restaurant review from lesson 12.4. Find a way to improve it. Use the Accuracy check, Register check, and the new language from this unit.

PAIR WORK PRACTICE (STUDENT A)

7.3   EXERCISE 2D   STUDENT A

Imagine you're talking to your partner on the phone. Say the news below, and your partner reacts. Then your partner says some news to you, and you react. Take turns.

1   My new job is really boring.

2   I'm having a cup of coffee.

3   It's my birthday today.

4   My dog is eating my lunch.

5   The people at my new college are friendly.

6   I'm on the subway.

8.3   EXERCISE 2D   STUDENT A

1   **Say the sentences below to your partner. Add information to explain or say more. Then your partner gives his or her opinion.**

- Basketball is/isn't my favorite sport. I mean, …
- I can/can't read music. It's difficult/easy. I mean, …
- I like / don't like art. I mean, …
- I think computer skills are important. I mean, …

> Basketball is my favorite sport. I mean, I can play really well, and it's fun.

> I don't like basketball. I think soccer is the best sport.

2   **Listen to your partner. Then give your opinion.**

10.3 EXERCISE 2D   STUDENT A

Your partner makes a suggestion. You say you can't and give a reason. Take turns.

Suggestion	Reason
have coffee now	(Your partner)
(Your partner)	go home at lunchtime
have a meeting on Monday	(Your partner)
(Your partner)	go to the supermarket
go shopping on Saturday	(Your partner)
(Your partner)	work late

> Let's have coffee now.

> I'm sorry, but I can't. I have to go to a meeting.

11.3 EXERCISE 2D   STUDENT A

1   **Ask your partner these questions. Listen to their answers. Then tell your partner the correct answers.**

Question	Answer
What was Leonardo DiCaprio's name in *Titanic*?	Jack Dawson
Where is the singer Carol Konka from?	Brazil
What country is *Crouching Tiger Hidden Dragon* from?	China
What was Elvis's last name?	Presley
What band is Chris Martin in?	Coldplay
What was the dog's name in *The Wizard of Oz*?	Toto

> What was Leonardo DiCaprio's name in *Titanic*?

> Uh, I think it was Jack. / Um, I have no idea.

> It was Jack Dawson.

2   **Answer your partner's questions. Use expressions of uncertainty for answers you don't know or are unsure about.**

This page is intentionally left blank

PAIR WORK PRACTICE (STUDENT B)

7.3   EXERCISE 2D   STUDENT B

Imagine you're talking to your partner on the phone. Your partner says some news to you, and you react. Then you say the news below, and your partner reacts. Take turns.

1 I'm cooking dinner.
2 I'm at a party on the beach.
3 I'm watching TV.

4 I'm working on Saturday and Sunday.
5 I have a new plane.
6 My train is three hours late.

8.3   EXERCISE 2D   STUDENT B

1 Listen to your partner. Then give your opinion.

> Basketball is my favorite sport. I mean, I can play really well, and it's fun.

> I don't like basketball. I think soccer is the best sport.

2 Say the sentences to your partner. Add information to explain or say more. Then your partner gives his or her opinion.

- Friday is/isn't my favorite day. I mean, …
- I like / don't like music. I mean, …
- I can/can't snowboard. It's difficult/easy. I mean, …
- I think good food is important. I mean, …

10.3 EXERCISE 2D   STUDENT B

You make a suggestion. Your partner says he/she can't and gives a reason. Take turns.

Suggestion	Reason for refusal
(Your partner)	go to a meeting
have lunch	(Your partner)
(Your partner)	go out
take a walk after work	(Your partner)
(Your partner)	study this weekend
watch a movie tonight	(Your partner)

> Let's have coffee now.

> I'm sorry, but I can't. I have to go to a meeting.

11.3 EXERCISE 2D   STUDENT B

1 Answer your partner's questions. Use expressions of uncertainty for answers you don't know or are unsure.

2 Ask your partner these questions. Listen to their answers. Then tell your partner the correct answers.

Question	Answer
What was Kate Winslet's name in *Titanic*?	Rose
Where is the band *Awesome City Club* from?	Japan
How many *Pirates of the Caribbean* movies was Johnny Depp in?	five
What is Shakira's last name?	Mebarak Ripoll
What band was John Lennon in?	The Beatles
What animals are in *101 Dalmatians*?	dogs

> What was Leonardo DiCaprio's name in *Titanic*?

> Uh, I think it was Jack. / Um, I have no idea.

> It was Jack Dawson.

EVOLVE

VIDEO RESOURCE BOOK

Janet Gokay and Noah Schwartzberg

1B

CAMBRIDGE
UNIVERSITY PRESS

This page is intentionally left blank

CONTENTS

ACKNOWLEDGMENTS

The authors and publishers acknowledge the following sources of copyright material and are grateful for the permissions granted. While every effort has been made, it has not always been possible to identify the sources of all the material used, or to trace all copyright holders. If any omissions are brought to our notice, we will be happy to include the appropriate acknowledgments on reprinting and in the next update to the digital edition, as applicable.

Key: B = Below, BR = Below Right, CL = Centre Left, CR = Centre Right, T = Top, TL = Top Left, TR = Top Right.

Photograph

The following photographs are sourced from Getty Images:

Video Resource Book: p.25 (TL): Peopleimages/E+; p.25 (TC): Kohei Hara/Taxi Japan; p.25 (TR): LisaValder/E+; p.29: Jessica Peterson; p.32: Klaus Vedfelt/DigitalVision; p.33 (TL): Zsolt Hlinka/Moment; p.33 (TC): M Swiet Productions/Moment; p.33 (TR): Matteo Colombo/Moment Open; p.34 (TL): Vitaliy Vilshanetskyy/EyeEm; p.34 (TC): Stephen Yelverton Photography/Moment; p.34 (TR): Ivan/Moment; p.34 (BL): Alexander Spatari/Moment; p.34 (BC): RebeccaAng/RooM; p.34 (BR): Matt Champlin/Moment; p.36: Thamrongpat Theerathammakom/EyeEm; p.37 (TL): Thomas Roche/Moment Open; p.37 (TR): Larry Gloth/Moment; p.37 (BL): Johnathan Ampersand Esper; p.38: Marc Romanelli/Blend Images; p.40: Hiroyuki Matsumoto/Photographer's Choice; p.41 (L): Teresa Recena/EyeEm; p.41 (C): Jose Luis Pelaez Inc/Blend Images; p.41 (R): aluxum/E+; p.43 (CL): Massimiliano Clari/EyeEm; p.43 (CR): Lew Robertson/Photodisc; p.43 (B): studiocasper/iStock/Getty Images Plus; p.45: franckreporter/E+; p.47 (T): Studio Omg/EyeEm; p.47 (CL): Mark Watts/EyeEm; p.47 (CR): Nodar Chenishev/EyeEm; p.61 (TL): Jupiterimages/Stockbyte; p.61 (TR): Tetra Images; p.61 (CL): andresr/E+; p.61 (CR): gawrav/E+; p.63 (T): Ty Milford; p.63 (CL): Hero Images; p.63 (CR): Jim Arbogast/Photodisc; p.64 (TL): Tom Werner/DigitalVision; p.64 (TR): RyanJLane/E+; p.64 (BL): RichLegg/E+; p.64 (BR): pahham/iStock; p.65 (TL): Cimmerian/E+; p.65 (TC): istanbulimage/E+; p.65 (TR): penguenstok/E+; p.65 (CL): evemilla/E+; p.65 (C): Florian Haas/EyeEm; p.65 (CR): Mika Mika/Moment; p.65 (BL): abzee/E+; p.65 (BC): Nicholas Eveleigh/Photodisc; p.65 (BR): Korkusung/iStock Editorial; p.67 (L): Petri Artturi Asikainen/Taxi Japan; p.65 (R): Petri Artturi Asikainen/Taxi Japan; p.68: Westend61; p.69 (TL): Hero Images; p.69 (TC): Martine Feiereisen/EyeEm; p.69 (TR): Steve Debenport/E+; p.69 (CL): Westend61; p.69 (C): svetikd/E+; p.69 (CR): Elyse Lewin/Stockbyte; p.72 (TL): Bussara T./EyeEm; p.72 (TC): Bill Boch/Photographer's Choice RF; p.72 (TR): Anton Vorozcov/EyeEm; p.72 (CL): Thai Yuan Lim/EyeEm; p.72 (CR): fancy.yan/Moment. **Videos:** U10: Nataliya Petrova/NurPhoto; MamiGibbs/Moment; Westend61; Maskot; Maria Moratti/Contigo/Getty Images News; Maksym Azovtsev/iStock/Getty Images Plus; PYMCA/Universal Images Group; Korkusung/iStock Editorial/Getty Images Plus; SeanPavonePhoto/iStock Editorial/Getty Images Plus; Petri Artturi Asikainen/Taxi Japan; T.Matsuda/DigitalVision; oneinchpunch/iStock/Getty Images Plus; Photo and Co/DigitalVision; rolf bruderer/Corbis; Jeremy Woodhouse/Blend Images; Pollyana FMS/Moment; Michael Niamut/Eyeem; Dennis Ncube/EyeEM; milanvirijevic/E+; Adam Hester/Blend Images; MStudioImages/iStock/Getty Images Plus; Satoshi Kawase/Moment Open; U12: YINJIA PAN/Moment; Pinghung Chen/EyeEm; gollykim/iStock/Getty Images Plus; Flash Parker/Moment Open; cougarsan/iStock/Getty Images Plus; Danita Delimont/Gallo Images; Stella Kalinina/Blend Images; Ronnie Kaufman/Larry Hirshowitz/Blend Images; Emely/Image Source; JGI/Jamie Grill/Blend Images.

Video

The following videos are sourced from Getty Images:

E7: Schroptschop/Vetta; Scott Mcpartland/Image Bank Film; Chuck and Sarah Fishbein/Iconica Video; U8: mgost/Creatas Video; Wehrwolf/Creatas Video+/Getty Images Plus; FatCamera/Creatas Video; shironosov/Creatas Video+/Getty Images Plus; petrunine/Creatas Video+/Getty Images Plus; smart_design/Creatas Video; konstantynov/Creatas Video; Brad Kremer/Photodisc; saskami/Creatas Video; Caiafilm/Creatas Video; Iksndr/Creatas Video; viafilms/Creatas Video; EmirMemedovski/Creatas Video; shih-wei/Creatas Video+; helivideo/Creatas Video+; MasterShot/Vetta; DGLimages/Creatas Video+; Silvestre Garcia - IntuitivoFilms/DigitalVision; monkeybusinessimages/ Creatas Video+; dubassy/Creatas Video+/Getty Images Plus; SVTeam/Creatas Video+; mgost/Vetta; U10: monkeybusinessimages/Creatas Video+; sisterspro/Creatas Video+; Alan Becker Productions/Verve; franckreporter/Vetta; Rocketclips/Verve+; Gkinion/Creatas Video; SimonSkafar/Vetta; Betsie

Van Der Meer/DigitalVision; ReeldealHD Ltd/Verve+; Anchiy/Creatas Video; Caiafilm; Edward Berthelot/Getty Images Entertainment Video; monkeybusinessimages/Creatas Video+/Getty Images Plus; U12: andresr/Creatas Video; Kosamtu/Vetta; tawattiw/Creatas Video; jessikla/Creatas Video; Slerpy/Creatas Video; andjic/Creatas Video; Nanhatai8/Creatas Video; Cameron Spencer/Getty Images Editorial Footage; Wavebreakmedia/Creatas Video+/Getty Images Plus; silverkblack/Creatas Video+/Getty Images Plus; FilmColoratStudio/Vetta; shironosov/Creatas Video+/Getty Images Plus.

Audio

The following musical clips are sourced from Getty Images:

E7 & E8: alexandru grigoriev/SoundExpress; E9: Kostya Leontovich / SoundExpress; E10: Gustav Eriksson/SoundExpress; E11: Sergey Sereda/SoundExpress; E12: frobisher/SoundExpress; U8: Alekss Hercbergs/SoundExpress; U10: Oleksandr Seletskyy/SoundExpress; AGUETTA/SoundExpress; U12: Brion Kennedy/SoundExpress; Alexandre Pier Federici/SoundExpress; Claudia Oblënder/SoundExpress.

Audio production by CityVox, New York.

Commissioned videos by People's TV.

BEFORE YOU WATCH

A **PAIR WORK** **Look at the pictures. Discuss the questions with a partner.**

Photo albums

1 Where do you keep your photos?
2 Do you have many photos of your family?
3 Do you have photos that are many years old?

B **How do you answer the phone in English? Complete the chart. Then compare with a partner.**

Answering the phone	Asking people how they are
Hi!	How's it going?

C **PREDICT** **Look at the pictures from the video. Answer the questions.**

1 Where is Christina?
2 What is she doing?
3 Who is calling Christina?
4 What kind of station is this?

WHILE YOU WATCH

A Check your answers to exercise C on page 25. Were your predictions correct?

B How do Christina and her mother answer the phone? How do they ask how people are? Check (✓) the phrases you hear.

☐ Hi, Mom. ☐ Hello, Mom.
☐ Oh, Chrissy! Hello! ☐ Hey, Chrissy!
☐ How are you, honey? ☐ How's it going?

C How do Christina and her mother end their phone calls? Check (✓) the phrases you hear.

☐ Uh, Mom. Marina is waiting for me. ☐ Good-bye, Mother.
☐ Call me in an hour, OK? ☐ OK, good. Talk to you later, OK?
☐ Oh, yes, sure … OK, bye! ☐ Fine, Chrissy. Bye-bye.

WHILE YOU WATCH

D **Complete the sentences with the present continuous forms of the verbs in parentheses.**

First Phone Call

1 What _____ you _____ (do)?

2 I _____ (finish) work for the day.

3 Marina _____ _____ (wait) for me at dance class.

4 _____ you _____ (make) the photo album for your father?

Second Phone Call

5 Yes, OK. Mom, I'm _____ (work) on it, but there are hundreds of photos.

6 Oh, Marina is _____ (come).

7 Um, the bus is _____ (come), too.

E **Who says the sentences in exercise D? Write *C* (Christina) or *M* (Mom).**

1 _____   3 _____   5 _____   7 _____

2 _____   4 _____   6 _____

F **Circle the responses you hear to complete the sentences.**

1 **Chrissy** Hi, Mom.

 Mom Oh, Chrissy! Hello! *How's it going / How are you, honey*?

2 **Mom** Oh, I'm sorry. Is this a bad time to call?

 Chrissy *No, no. / It's not bad.* … Well, maybe.

3 **Mom** Um … I have one question.

 Chrissy *Yes / What*, Mom?

4 **Chrissy** Call me in 20 minutes, OK?

 Mom *That's fine / Oh, yes, sure.*

5 **Mom** Is Marina with you now?

 Chrissy No. *I can talk / I have a little time.*

6 **Chrissy** Can we call you from home? … *Yes. / OK, good.* Talk to you later, OK?

 Mom OK, Chrissy. *Bye-bye / Good-bye.*

Photocopiable © Cambridge University Press 2019   Drama   27

AFTER YOU WATCH

A   **What do you remember? Answer the questions.**

1   What does Christina's mother want?

2   Where is Christina's daughter?

3   What transportation does Christina take?

B   PAIR WORK   **Discuss the questions with a partner.**

1   Christina's mom calls her "Chrissy." What do people in your family call you?
2   What do your friends call you?
3   What do you call your friends and family members?

C   PAIR WORK   **Imagine you're busy. You get a call. What do you say? Role play the situation with a partner.**

A

Hi! How's it going?

B

Sorry, I'm busy.

OK, but I'm (eating dinner).

Sorry, this is a bad time for me.

Can I call you later?

A

Oh, OK.

That's OK.

That's fine.

No problem.

BEFORE YOU WATCH

A   **What can you do well? What can't you do well? Complete the chart. Compare with a partner.**

Can do well	Can't do well
read	swim
play the guitar	read music

> I can read well. I can't swim well.

> I can't read music well, but I can play the guitar pretty well!

B   **PAIR WORK**   **Discuss the questions.**

1   Are you busy or not too busy? Do you like to be busy?
2   Do you ever feel that you have too much to do?
3   What can you do if you are too busy?
4   What do you want someone to do for you?

> I am really busy. I go to work – and I come to English class! I have too much to do.

> What do you think you can do about it?

> Maybe someone else can do my laundry!

C   **PREDICT**   **Look at the pictures from the video. Answer the questions.**

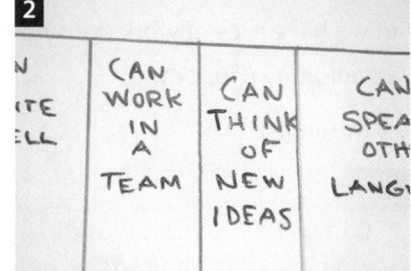

CAN WORK IN A TEAM   CAN THINK OF NEW IDEAS   CAN SPEA OTH LANG

1   Where are Christina and Noemi? _____
2   Who is writing on the board? _____
3   Who is looking at a laptop? _____
4   What is Noemi doing in picture 3? _____

WHILE YOU WATCH

A   **Check your answers to exercise C on page 29. Were your predictions correct?**

B   **Circle the correct answers.**

1   Noemi has a problem with her *hand / back*.
2   Christina is looking for *help / work*.
3   Noemi asks, "What do you think about *Robert / Hank*?"
4   Teresa doesn't like *homework / teamwork*.
5   Robert *can / can't* communicate well.
6   *Noemi / Christina* says, "But we have a lot of work right now."
7   Christina says, "Tomorrow's *Saturday / Sunday*."

C   **What can they do? Check (✓) the skills.**

Names	Can communicate	Can write well	Can work in a team	Can think of new ideas	Can speak other languages	Other
Hank						
Teresa						
Robert						*good* with numbers

WHILE YOU WATCH

D   **Match the sentences (1–7) with the responses (a–g).**

1   Are you OK now? __b__
2   So, what are you working on? _____
3   What do you think about Hank? _____
4   OK, Robert. Can he communicate and write well? _____
5   Great! Not for this job, but it's a fun skill. _____
6   Ugh! I work all the time! _____
7   My back! I need a break! _____

a   I agree!
b   Yeah. My back is a problem sometimes.
c   You can do a lot of things … but you can't do everything.
d   Well, Hank can't write well.
e   Yes, he can!
f   Well, I'm looking for help.
g   Yes, you do. Hey, tomorrow's Saturday.

E   **Look at the sentences in exercise D again. Who says the sentences? Write the letters and numbers next to the correct names.**

1   Christina: __1__
2   Noemi: __b__

F   Circle **the correct answers.**

1   Noemi's doctor is _____ Christina's office.
   a   near   b   far from
2   Christina is _____ for help.
   a   looking   b   asking
3   Teresa _____ in a team.
   a   can work   b   can't work
4   _____ can speak three languages.
   a   Teresa   b   Hank
5   Robert is good with _____.
   a   numbers   b   letters
6   _____ plays the guitar.
   a   Hank   b   Robert
7   Noemi has ten _____ on her phone.
   a   emails   b   text messages

AFTER YOU WATCH

A   **What do you remember? Answer the questions.**

1   Who does Christina really like for the job?

_____

2   Who is working a lot these days?

_____

3   What does Teresa say she doesn't like?

_____

4   What fun skill does Robert have?

_____

5   Who is texting Noemi?

_____

6   Who does Noemi work for?

_____

7   Who is the best person for the job?

_____

B   **Look at the skills charts in exercise C on page 30. Make notes about other important skills. Then discuss the questions with a partner.**

1   Which skills are important for Christina's job?
2   Who is best for the job?
3   Think of a job you have or want. What skills do you need for it?

BEFORE YOU WATCH

A **PAIR WORK** Which of these places do you want to visit? What can you see and do in each place? You can look up information about the places.

New York City, U.S.

Tulum, Mexico

Costa Rica

> I want to go to New York City. I can go to a museum there.

> Really? I want to go to a beach in Mexico. I like to swim in the ocean.

B **PAIR WORK** What are your plans for the weekend? Complete the chart. Share with a partner.

Activity	have to / need to	want to
clean my apartment	✗	
watch a movie		✗

> I have to clean my apartment this weekend. I want to watch a movie. How about you?

C **PREDICT** Look at the picture of Noemi. What is she doing? Discuss with a partner.

WHILE YOU WATCH

A Check your answer to exercise C on page 33. Was your prediction correct?

B (Circle) the correct answers.

1 Noemi is _____.
   a happy   b tired

2 Noemi is thinking about _____.
   a phone   b vacations

3 Noemi and Christina are looking at _____ guides.
   a park   b travel

4 Noemi doesn't know _____ to go.
   a where   b when

5 Noemi wants to go somewhere _____.
   a near   b far

6 Noemi can _____ to the Adirondacks.
   a fly   b drive

7 _____ don't usually work in the Adirondacks.
   a Cars   b Phones

8 Hotels in the Adirondacks _____ have phones.
   a do   b don't

9 _____ calls Noemi.
   a Christina   b Rick

10 Noemi needs a _____.
   a vacation   b phone

C Check (✓) the places people mention. Then write the letter of each picture next to the name.

☐ 1 Florence, Italy _____
☐ 2 Las Vegas _____
☐ 3 Miami _____
☐ 4 New York City _____
☐ 5 the Adirondacks _____
☐ 6 the Grand Canyon (national park) _____

WHILE YOU WATCH

D (Circle) the words you hear to complete the sentences.

1 Not today! I'm thinking about *work / vacations*!

2 You need a vacation from your *work / phone*!

3 Hi, Eduardo! *How are you? / How's it going?*

4 I *want / need* to plan a vacation, but I don't know *where / when* to go.

5 She needs to go to a place with no *hotels / phones*.

6 Yeah, it's near. And yes, you can *fly / drive*. You *have to / don't have to* fly.

7 *Laptops / Phones* don't usually work there.

8 She's working too *hard / much*, Eduardo.

9 Yeah, I can see. Well, she *can / can't* go to the Adirondacks …

E **Match the pictures (A–E) with the sentences you hear (1–5).**

1 OK. Where can you go near here? _____

2 No phones? Hmm. _____

3 What is it, Rick? _____

4 She's working too hard, Eduardo. _____

5 I have the perfect place! _____

F **Look again at exercise E. Who says each sentence? Write *N* (Noemi), *C* (Christina), or *E* (Eduardo).**

1 OK. Where can you go near here? _____

2 No phones? Hmm. _____

3 What is it, Rick? _____

4 She's working too hard, Eduardo. _____

5 I have the perfect place! _____

AFTER YOU WATCH

A **PAIR WORK** What do you remember? Answer the questions with a partner.

1 Why is Noemi stressed?

2 Why does Christina say, "You need a vacation … from your phone!"?

3 How do the friends know Noemi needs a vacation?

4 Do you want to go to the same place Noemi does? Why or why not?

B **PAIR WORK** Eduardo says about Noemi, "She can go to the Adirondacks, and her phone can stay at home." Answer these questions. Discuss with a partner.

1 Do you like this idea?

2 When do you leave your phone at home?

3 Do you think it's hard or easy to leave your phone at home?

4 Do you think Noemi is happy or sad about this idea?

🎭 Drama

BEFORE YOU WATCH

A **Match the words (1–5) with the definitions (a–e).**

1 to stop (somewhere) _____
2 to stay home _____
3 That's too bad. _____
4 outside _____
5 fall _____

a I'm sorry. That's not good.
b outdoors; not inside a building
c to not leave your house
d the season between summer and winter
e to stay in a place for a short time

B **Complete the sentences with the words from exercise A.**

1 **A** Are you going to go to the concert tomorrow?
  B No, I'm going _____. I have a lot of work.

2 **A** I can't go to the concert tomorrow. I have to work.
  B _____. It's going to be fun!

3 **A** Where are you going to eat lunch today – in the cafeteria?
  B No. It's a beautiful day. I'm going to sit _____!

4 **A** Can we _____ at the bookstore for a minute? I need to get a book.
  B Sure, no problem.

5 **A** What's your favorite season?
  B Oh, _____! I love seeing the trees change colors.

C **Look at the pictures of people in the Adirondack Mountains in the fall.**
  Check (✓) the clothing you see.

☐ boots
☐ coat
☐ dress
☐ hat
☐ jeans
☐ pants
☐ shirt
☐ shoes
☐ shorts
☐ skirt
☐ sweater
☐ T-shirt

WHILE YOU WATCH

A   **Check (✓) the clothes Eduardo and Noemi talk about.**

☐ boots   ☐ shirt
☐ coat   ☐ shoes
☐ dress   ☐ shorts
☐ hat   ☐ skirt
☐ jeans   ☐ sweater
☐ pants   ☐ T-shirt

B   **What is Noemi going to do on her vacation? Check *going to* or *not going to* to make the sentences true.**

		going to	not going to	
	1			stay in a small hotel.
	2			sleep a lot.
	3			eat good food.
	4			watch TV.
	5			read.
Noemi is …	6			walk a lot.
	7			run in the park.
	8			sit outside.
	9			sleep in the sun.
	10			drive to the Adirondacks.
	11			talk on the phone.

WHILE YOU WATCH

C   (Circle) the words you hear to complete the sentences.

1   I'm *going / go* to stay in a small hotel.

2   What else are you going to *do / see*?

3   I'm going to *sit / sleep* a lot, eat good food, and *read / buy* books.

4   Are you going *go / to go* outside, too?

5   It's cold in the *winter / fall*.

6   A good pair of *boots / shoes* is fine.

7   Oh, yeah, you mean the Friday night *food / taco* trucks?

8   So, *next / this* Friday?

9   Great. But I'm *to see / going to see* you before then, right?

10 Enjoy your *work / workout*.

D   **Listen for these sentences. Is the person making a suggestion (M), accepting a suggestion (A), or refusing a suggestion (R)? Write *M*, *A*, or *R*.**

1   Yes, but you can walk. Bring long pants – a sweater or two. _____

2   OK. What about boots? _____

3   No, you don't need boots. A good pair of shoes is fine. _____

4   Yeah, but you can stop on the way, have lunch. _____

5   OK, great. Thank you! _____

6   So, do you want to go? _____

7   I can't. _____

8   So, next Friday? _____

9   Great. But I'm going to see you before then, right? _____

AFTER YOU WATCH

A PAIR WORK Write notes on your answers to the questions. Then discuss with a partner.

1 Does Noemi's vacation sound fun to you? Why or why not?

2 What things does Noemi talk about that you like to do?

3 What do you like to do on a vacation?

4 What do you not like to do on a vacation?

B PAIR WORK Think of your next vacation. Where are you going to go? When? With who? What are you going to do? What clothes do you need to take? Complete the chart and then ask and answer questions with a partner.

Where	When	With who	What you are going to do	Clothes

I'm going to New York City in August!

Cool! Are you going with your family?

No, I'm going alone – but I'm staying with a friend.

So, what are you going to do?

Well, we're going to a concert in the park on Saturday …

Drama   EVOLVE 1 Episode 10

BEFORE YOU WATCH

A   **Look at the pictures and ⃝circle⃝ the correct answers.**

1   Where is Christina?
    a   She is at home.
    b   She is at the office.
2   Who is this?
    a   Christina's friend
    b   Christina's office assistant
3   Where was the phone?
    a   on the table
    b   in the box

4   What is Rick holding?
    a   a pizza
    b   coffee

5   What is funny?
    a   the party stuff
    b   the zoo

B   **Match the pictures (A–C) with the sentences (1–3). What do they have in common?**

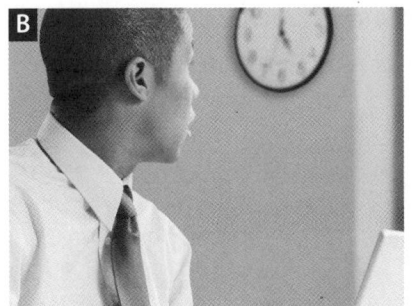

1   Time for a coffee break! _____
2   Oh! It's getting late. Time to go home. _____
3   Hard work makes me hungry. _____

C   PREDICT   **Where are Christina and Eduardo? What are they doing? What's in the box? Write your answers.**

_____
_____
_____
_____
_____
_____

WHILE YOU WATCH

A   Check your answers to exercise C on page 41. Were your predictions correct?

B   Check (✓) who does these things. Sometimes there is more than one answer.

Noemi

Rick

Christina

Eduardo

Who...	Noemi	Rick	Christina	Eduardo
1 needs help getting organized?				
2 arrives early?				
3 gives Eduardo coffee?				
4 dressed as a cat at an office party?				
5 is going to get Marina?				
6 is going to eat with Eduardo?				

C   Complete the conversation with the words you hear. What word does Christina use to show uncertainty? What word does she use to show surprise? What words does Eduardo use to show surprise?

Eduardo   Wow. There are a lot of things here. Where do I ¹_____?

Christina   Um … this ²_____?

…

Eduardo   Ha! Look at this! ³_____ this yours?

Christina   Oh! My ⁴_____ phone. Yes, it was.

Eduardo   Does it ⁵_____?

Christina   I don't ⁶_____ so.

D   Correct the words in bold. Then put the sentences in the correct order.

_____   Eduardo arrives **last**. _____

_____   Christina says she is going to get **Noemi**. _____

_____   Rick and Noemi **leave**. _____

_____   Christina wants to clean out her **bedroom**, and her friends are going to help her. _____

_____   Eduardo finds an old **toy** of Christina's. _____

_____   Rick, Noemi, and Eduardo decide to **go to a movie** together. _____

_____   **Rick** puts on a cat mask. _____

WHILE YOU WATCH

E   **Check (✓) the sentences that are true. Correct the false ones.**

☐ **1** Noemi arrives first. _____

☐ **2** Eduardo is late. _____

☐ **3** Noemi comes from the gym. _____

☐ **4** Rick is going to get a new office assistant. _____

☐ **5** Christina's phone was from 2004. _____

☐ **6** Christina's old office had a lot of parties. _____

☐ **7** Christina needs the green things. _____

☐ **8** Everyone is going to get dinner together. _____

F   **Complete the missing information with the words in the box.**

cats	gym	hungry	old	party	pizza

1 Eduardo was at the _____.

2 The _____ phone was Christina's.

3 The masks were from Christina's office _____.

4 Christina doesn't like _____.

5 Hard work makes Eduardo _____.

6 Next week, _____ for everyone!

G   **Complete the conversation. What word means something is delicious? What word means to stop and take a short rest? What do you like to do when you take a rest?**

Rick   Hey, everyone! Coffee ¹ _____?

Eduardo   ² _____. Great!

Rick   Here's ³ _____, Christina, and ⁴ _____, Eduardo.

Eduardo   Thanks! Now we're ⁵ _____ to go!

AFTER YOU WATCH

A   What do you think *Many hands make light work* means? Is there a similar expression in your country?

Thanks for helping me.

No problem. Many hands make light work!

B   What does Eduardo want to do with the phone? What does Christina want to do with the phone? What reasons do they give? Who do you think is right? Are you more like Christina or Eduardo?

C   Do you have a favorite possession you will never throw out? Why is it special?

D   PAIR WORK   Did you have a favorite toy or possession when you were little? Describe it for your partner.

I remember I had a … It was …

BEFORE YOU WATCH

A   Look at the pictures. Where are Eduardo, Christina, and Noemi? What is Eduardo eating? What is on the plate? What meal is it?

B   PAIR WORK   Put the words in order to make questions. Imagine you are Eduardo and answer the questions with the information from exercise A. Then ask and answer the questions with a partner. Use personal information.

1   today / What / eat / you / did / for breakfast / ?

_____

2   you / Did / drink/ coffee / today / any / ?

_____

3   you / Did / have / this morning / any / juice / ?

_____

4   you / eat / Did / fruit / any / today / ?

_____

C   What's *takeout*? Where do you get it? Do you ever get takeout? Why or why not?

D   PREDICT   Can you predict what's wrong with Rick?

WHILE YOU WATCH

A   **Check your answer to exercise D on page 45. Was your prediction correct?**

B   **Put the sentences in the order they happen in the video (1–7).**

_____ Noemi met Christina at the café.

_____ Rick ate takeout food.

_____ Christina arrived at the café.

_____ Rick went to the restroom.

_____ Eduardo and Rick played soccer.

_____ Noemi asked Rick to cook for them.

_____ Eduardo ate a pastry and drank coffee.

C   **Who says these sentences? Write *E* (Eduardo), *N* (Noemi), *R* (Rick), or *C* (Christina).**

1   Marina had a dance show at school last night. _____

2   You're a good mom. _____

3   We played until 10:30. _____

4   Well, I had some takeout last night. _____

5   I don't want to talk about it. _____

6   You need to eat simple food today. _____

7   How about a cheese and fruit plate? _____

8   I can't think about food right now. _____

9   My sister says "hi." _____

D   **Put the words in order to make questions. Ask and answer them with a partner.**

1   the friends / meet / Where / do / ?

_____

2   last night / Rick and Eduardo / What / did / play / ?

_____

3   Rick / Why / late / is / to breakfast / ?

_____

4   Rick / What / did / eat / last night / ?

_____

5   color / What / the sauce / was / ?

_____

6   was / What / the sauce / in / ?

_____

7   wrong / the chicken / What / was / with / ?

_____

WHILE YOU WATCH

E   **Complete the conversations with the words you hear. Which phrases offer food or drinks? Which phrases request food or drinks?**

1   **Noemi**   OK. [1]_____ _____ some water?

    Rick   Maybe.

2   **Christina**   Some [2]_____, and [3]_____ a banana?

    Rick   Uh, no rice, [4]_____.

    Christina   OK, some crackers then.

    Rick   OK. Crackers and [5]_____.

3   **Christina**   What [6]_____, Noemi?

    Noemi   Um, [7]_____ a cheese and [8]_____ plate?

F   **Read the sentences. Circle the actions that are correct for each person. There can be more than one correct answer for each person. Then compare with a partner.**

Rick …	Eduardo …	Christina …	Noemi …
ate warm chicken.	ate cold chicken.	went to a dance show last night.	texted Rick, but he didn't text back.
arrived at the café after his friends.	doesn't want any eggs.	texted Rick, but he didn't text back.	loves to cook.
has a message from his sister.	has a message from his sister.	offers Rick a fruit plate.	offers Rick some crackers and bananas.
thinks a dinner party is a great idea.	thinks a dinner party is a great idea.	feels tired.	says Rick can cook for them.

G   **Complete the conversation with the words in the box.**

bad	cold	eggs	hungry	idea	white

Eduardo   Ah … late night takeout. It's never a good [1]_____.

Rick   Yeah. The chicken was [2]_____. And the sauce … well, it was [3]_____.

Christina   Then why did you eat it?

Rick   I was [4]_____!

Christina   What was in it?

Rick   The sauce? I don't know. It was [5]_____ sauce.

Christina   So, milk, butter, maybe [6]_____? Or was it the chicken?

AFTER YOU WATCH

A   **Imagine who says these sentences. Write *E* (Eduardo), *N* (Noemi), *R* (Rick), or *C* (Christina).**

   1   I'm happy Eduardo's sister said "hi." _____

   2   I'm tired, so I'm going home to rest. _____

   3   Poor Rick. Now I know why he didn't text me back this morning! _____

   4   I'm going to tidy my apartment for the dinner party. _____

B   PAIR WORK   **Look at the answer to exercise A, number 1. Why do you think this person is happy? Then look at the answer to number 2. Why do you think this person is tired?**

C   PAIR WORK   **Think about a very good meal and a very bad meal you had at a restaurant. Take turns asking and answering the questions.**

   1   What did you eat?

   2   What did you drink?

   3   Who did you eat with?

   4   How much money did you spend?

   5   Was the food good or bad? Why?

D   **What makes a good meal? What makes a bad meal? Write notes.**

Good	Bad

E   **What is something you won't eat? Why?**

_____

_____

_____

_____

5 STEPS TO LEARN A NEW SKILL

BEFORE YOU WATCH

A **Look at the pictures. What do they all show?**

B **Read the definitions. Then unscramble the letters to make words to match them.**

1 i f x _____ to make a broken thing better

2 i l s k l _____ the ability to do an activity well

3 r p a t c e i c _____ to do something again and again to get better at it

4 a l g o _____ something you want to do with success in the future

5 r e t i _____ a thick, round piece of rubber that fits around a wheel

6 t s p e _____ one of the things you do to succeed at something

C PAIR WORK **Look at the activities in exercise A. What skill is the most difficult to learn? Discuss with a partner.**

D PREDICT **Look at the picture from the video. What are the people doing? What do you think the video is about? Make a prediction.**

a performing

b learning new skills

c the arts

WHILE YOU WATCH

A   Look at the pictures below and watch the video. Was your prediction correct?
    What is the video about?

B   According to the video, how many hours does it take to learn a new skill?

  1   Some people say _____ .

  2   Other people say _____ .

C   Complete the five steps to learn a new skill from the video.

  Step 1   Choose _____ .

  Step 2   Think about _____ .

  Step 3   Find time _____ .

  Step 4   Think about _____ .

  Step 5   And finally, _____ .

D   Match the phrases in each column to make sentences from the video.

  1   It's important _____   **a**   20 hours or more.

  2   To learn how to paint, _____   **b**   and more quickly the next.

  3   Speak slowly one day _____   **c**   "Learn to fix things."

  4   It's good to practice _____   **d**   to practice every day.

  5   Don't say, _____   **e**   but in a different way.

  6   Practice for _____   **f**   in the morning.

  7   Do the same thing _____   **g**   you need to learn about colors.

Documentary   EVOLVE 1   Unit 8

WHILE YOU WATCH

E   **Watch the video and write the missing words.**

¹ _____ are things we can or can't do,
like ² _____ , ride a bike, or speak another
³ _____ . Some people say it takes 10,000 hours
to ⁴ _____ _____
_____ . That's ⁵ _____ an hour a day
for 27 years! But there's good news. Other people say
⁶ _____ _____ learn a new
skill in just 20 hours!

F   **What do you remember about learning a new skill? Circle the correct answer
to complete the steps. Then watch the video again to check your answers.**

1   Choose _____ goal.
    a an easy   **b** a small

2   Think about what parts of the skill are _____
    to learn.
    a hard   **b** important

3   Find _____ to practice.
    a time   **b** space

4   Think about _____ to practice.
    a what   **b** how

5   And finally, practice for _____ hours.
    a 20   **b** 10,000

G   **Answer the questions based on the information in the video.**

1   What example does the video give of a small goal?

_____

2   What do you need to learn about to paint?

_____

3   What do you need to learn about to make cool movies?

_____

4   How often should you practice a skill?

_____

5   What two things help your brain remember?

_____

AFTER YOU WATCH

A   Look at the pictures. Are these skills? Why or why not?

B   PAIR WORK   Look at the skills in the box. Which are easy? Which are hard? Put them in order from easiest to hardest to learn. Then compare your list with your partner. Discuss how your lists are similar and different.

cooking	learning a new language	learning to drive	playing a musical instrument
riding a bicycle	singing	swimming	yoga

C   PAIR WORK   Choose one skill you can do well. What steps do people need to take to learn this skill? How should they practice? Explain the steps to your partner.

BEFORE YOU WATCH

A   **Write the words in the box below the correct pictures.**

> boots   coat   headphones   scarf   skirt   suit   sweater   sunglasses

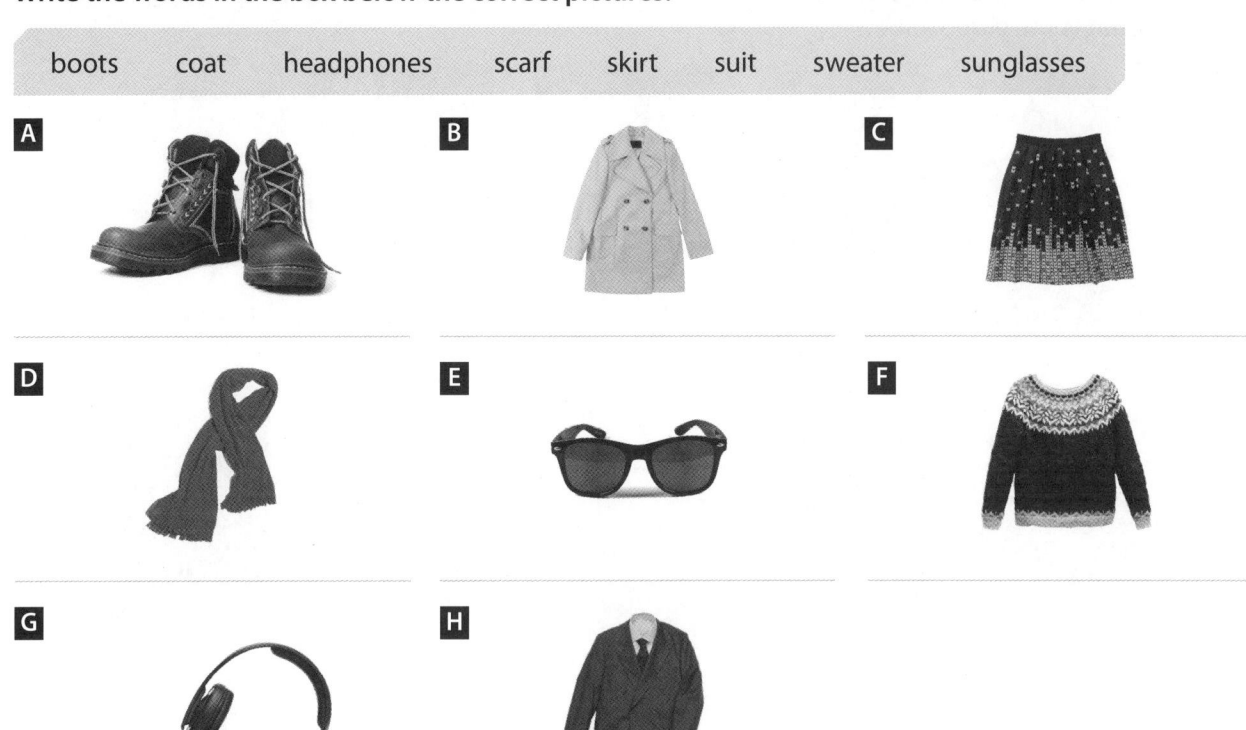

A _____

B _____

C _____

D _____

E _____

F _____

G _____

H _____

B   **Complete the sentences with the correct words from exercise A.**

1   A _____ goes around a person's neck.

2   People wear _____ to listen to their favorite music.

3   Some people wear a _____ to a job interview.

4   _____ can keep your feet dry.

5   A _____ hangs from the waist and down over the legs.

6   A _____ is a piece of clothing you wear above the waist to keep warm.

7   People wear _____ to keep the sun out of their eyes.

8   People wear a _____ over their clothes when it's cold outside.

C   PAIR WORK   **Choose a word from the box that best describes your style. Explain your choice to a partner.**

> athletic   casual   fashionable   formal   fun

D   PREDICT   **Look at the picture. What does it show? What do you think the video is about? Make a prediction.**

a   a festival   b   style   c   traditions

WHILE YOU WATCH

A   Look at the pictures and watch the video. Was your prediction in exercise D on page 65 correct? What is the video about?

B   Ⓒircle the words you hear in the video.

jeans	dress	headphones	sweatshirt
backpack	scarf	bow tie	boots
jacket	shirt	sunglasses	shoes

C   What do people wear in different countries? Check (✓) the correct boxes.

	Cameroon	Russia	Slovenia	Japan	U.S.	Italy
coats, boots, and scarves						
a shirt and pants						
fun suits						
sweaters over skirts						
a head scarf						
a backpack and a bike						

D   Answer the questions. Write the names of cities or countries.

   1   Where is the street style very casual? _____

   2   Where can you see lots of different street styles? _____

   3   Where else is the street style like San Francisco? _____

   4   Where do people wear hats? _____

WHILE YOU WATCH

E   **Watch the video and complete the missing words.**

In Japan, well, people wear lots of different things! These styles look ¹ _____, but they have one thing in common: ² _____! Actually, on the ³ _____ of Harajuku in ⁴ _____, you can see all kinds of street style: from ⁵ _____ sweaters over skirts, to ⁶ _____ suits, and ⁷ _____ dresses.

F   **What do you remember about street style?** Circle **the correct answer to complete the sentences. Then watch the video again to check your answers.**

1   Street style is _____.

   a   how people show their true style   **b**   just what people wear on the street

2   In Japan, some people wear _____.

   a   sunglasses and headphones   **b**   big sweaters over skirts

3   Street style is _____.

   a   often very casual   **b**   often very formal

4   Street style in different countries is _____.

   a   completely different   **b**   sometimes the same

G   **Answer the questions based on the information in the video.**

1   What do the different styles in Japan have in common?

_____

2   In what three places is street style similar?

_____

3   What items of clothing do you see the most in the video?

_____

AFTER YOU WATCH

A   PAIR WORK   What did you think of the street styles in the video? What place do you think has the best street style? Explain your opinion to a partner.

B   PAIR WORK   Imagine you are at the following places. What do you wear? Compare with your partner. Are your styles similar?

dinner with friends	home	important meeting at work
outdoor music festival	tourist site	

C   What do you think about crazy street styles? Are they cool? What crazy street style do you want to try?

WHY DID THEY TAKE THAT PICTURE?

BEFORE YOU WATCH

A   **Look at the pictures. What do they show? Read the categories. Write the letter of the category that best fits each picture. Some pictures can have more than one category.**

a   a special event or memory

b   a job well done or a special achievement

c   showing how to do something

B   **PAIR WORK** **Use your phone and look for a picture that you want to show to a partner. Then ask each other these questions.**

1   What is it a picture of?

2   Why did you take it?

3   Why do you think it's a good picture?

4   Do you like to look at other people's pictures? Why or why not?

C   **PREDICT** **Look at the picture. What is the woman doing? What do you think the video is about? Circle your prediction.**

a   cell phones are everywhere

b   apps for healthy eating

c   taking pictures of food

WHILE YOU WATCH

A   Watch the video. What is it about? Was your prediction correct? What amount of people do this?

B   Put the events in the order they happen in the video (1–5).

_____   A man makes a cooking video.

_____   Three young women take a selfie at a waterfall.

_____   A woman blows out birthday candles.

_____   A happy group of friends take a selfie at a restaurant while eating dinner together.

_____   Two kids show orange slices for smiles.

C   Match the activities (1–3) with the percentages (a–c) according to the information presented
in the video.

1 people who take pictures of food they cooked _____	**a** 20%	
2 people who take pictures of food at special events _____	**b** 22%	
3 people who take pictures of food at a restaurant _____	**c** 33%	

D   Read the activities. Who do they describe? Check (✓) the correct boxes.

Who ...	Karl and Cindy	Dan	Donna	Steve
looks at pictures to remember a trip?				
has their own show?				
took pictures of the food he ate?				
photographed someone's birthday?				
went to Singapore last summer?				
went to a new restaurant?				

Photocopiable © Cambridge University Press 2019   EVOLVE 1   Unit 12

WHILE YOU WATCH

E   **According to the video, what are the three reasons why people take pictures of their food?**

_____

_____

F   **Watch the video and complete the missing words.**

Larissa took this video of a delicious ¹_____ she made. Then she
²_____ it to her ³_____ _____ page. Some
people, like Steve, like to ⁴_____ so much, they have their own video show.
Steve made this video to ⁵_____ people how to make a ⁶_____
for dinner.

G   Correct the mistake in each sentence to make it true.

1   About 25% of people take pictures of food.

_____

2   When Dan went to Singapore, he enjoyed taking pictures at the night market.

_____

3   Most families have famous food photos.

_____

4   Some people watch videos to teach what they know.

_____

5   People take pictures of their families because they feel good about it.

_____

AFTER YOU WATCH

A   **What people from the video are most likely to say the sentences? Write *Dan*, *Donna*, *Larissa*, *Karl*, or *Steve*.**

1   I hope my mom enjoyed her party. _____

2   Breakfast is my favorite meal of the day. _____

3   Over 10,000 people follow my videos. _____

4   I love to travel and try new food. Next summer I'm going to Russia. I can't wait! _____

5   I go to a new restaurant about once a month. _____

B   PAIR WORK   **Choose one of the pictures and imagine you took it. Do not tell your partner which one. Ask and answer the questions. Guess which picture your partner "took."**

Was the restaurant busy?   What did you have to drink?   Was the food expensive?

Who did you eat with?   Did you have a reservation?   Will you go back to that restaurant?

> Was the restaurant busy?

> No, it wasn't busy. There were only eight people eating there.

C   PAIR WORK   **What kind of food do you like? What kind of restaurant do you like to eat at? Write notes about your preferences. Share with your partner. Then make restaurant recommendations to each other.**

Type of food: _____

Style of restaurant: _____

Price: _____

Restaurant recommendation for your partner: _____

Photocopiable © Cambridge University Press 2019

EVOLVE

WORKBOOK

Samuela Eckstut

1B

This page is intentionally left blank

CONTENTS

1   VOCABULARY: Activities around the house

A   **Cross out the words that do <u>not</u> complete the sentences.**

1	I clean _____ on the weekend.	the bathroom	the kitchen	~~my hair~~
2	We cook _____ every day.	coffee	dinner	breakfast
3	He washes _____ at night.	the computer	his hair	the dog
4	She brushes _____ in the morning.	her hair	her bed	her teeth
5	I take _____ every morning.	a bath	my room	a shower
6	They do _____ in the evening.	their breakfast	the dishes	their homework
7	You help _____ a lot.	your friends	your home	your mother

2   GRAMMAR: Present continuous statements

A   **Write the –ing form of the verbs.**

1 chat   *chatting*
2 do   _____
3 eat   _____
4 get   _____
5 go   _____
6 have   _____
7 play   _____
8 run   _____
9 shop   _____
10 study   _____
11 take   _____
12 work   _____

B **Complete the sentences with the present continuous form of the verbs in parentheses ( ).**

1 I'm chatting _____ (chat) on the phone right now.

2 We _____ (do) the dishes in the kitchen.

3 Sara and Tomas are at a store. They _____ (shop) for new furniture.

4 Riu is in the bathroom. He _____ (take) a shower.

5 The girls are in the park. They _____ (run).

6 This game isn't boring. We _____ (have) fun.

7 The children are in bed, but they _____ (get) up now.

8 I'm in the kitchen. I _____ (eat) lunch.

3 GRAMMAR AND VOCABULARY

A **Complete the sentences with the affirmative (+) or negative (–) form of the present continuous.**

1 I usually take a shower at 7:30 a.m. It's 9:00 now.
I'm not taking _____ a shower right now.

2 Sandra doesn't cook lunch on weekdays. It's noon on Tuesday. Sandra _____ lunch at the moment.

3 Benjamin and Deb do the dishes after dinner. It's after dinner. They _____ the dishes.

4 Harry always brushes his teeth after he eats. It's after lunch. He _____ his teeth now.

5 Eva always helps her parents on the weekend. It's Saturday. She _____ her parents right now.

6 My family and I never clean our house on a weekday. It's Monday. We _____ our house.

B **Circle the correct words.**

1 I sometimes *take* / *am taking* a bath at night.

2 Ruiz *doesn't cook* / *isn't cooking* dinner right now.

3 The students often *do* / *are doing* their homework before class.

4 I always *am brushing* / *brush* my teeth in the morning and at night.

5 My family and I never *do* / *are doing* the dishes together.

6 Katya *cleans* / *is cleaning* her room right now.

C **Look at the sentences in exercise 3B. Then write what you are doing (or not doing) right now.**

1 _____ I'm not taking a bath right now. _____

2 _____

3 _____

4 _____

5 _____

6 _____

TEXTING ON THE RUN

1 VOCABULARY: Transportation

A **Match the questions (1–6) with the answers (a–f).**

1 Are you driving to work? _____c_____
2 Are you walking to work? _____
3 Are you at the movie theater? _____
4 What are you studying? _____
5 Are you coming home now? _____
6 Where are you riding your bike? _____

a Yes. I'm waiting for Tom.
b No. My office isn't near my house.
c Yes, I am. I drive every day.
d I'm riding it to the park.
e Yes, but I'm shopping in the mall first.
f I'm not studying right now. I'm reading.

2 GRAMMAR: Present continuous questions

A **Read the words and write questions.**

1 you / do / homework / right now?   _Are you doing your homework right now?_
2 your friends / play / soccer / right now?
3 your friend / send / you / a text message?
4 you and your friends / learn / English?
5 you / listen / to music / right now?

B **Answer the questions so they are true for you.**

1 _____Yes, I am._____
2 _____
3 _____
4 _____
5 _____

C **Read the short conversations. Write the questions for B.**

1 A Lisa isn't waiting for her husband.

 B *Who is she waiting for?*

 A She's waiting for her brother.

2 A I'm not going to work right now.

 B _____

 A I'm going to the supermarket.

3 A Yoko's in the kitchen.

 B _____

 A She's studying for her exam. And drinking coffee!

4 A The boys are carrying some big bags.

 B _____

 A Because they're helping their aunt.

5 A I'm helping my daughter with her homework.

 B _____

 A Because she has an exam on Friday.

6 A My children are in the park.

 B _____

 A No, not soccer. They're playing basketball.

3 GRAMMAR AND VOCABULARY

A **You are on a train. People are talking on their cell phones. Write present continuous questions for the answers. Use the words in the box.**

go	on the bus	ride your bike	~~take the train~~	wait for your friend	walk

1 A *Are you taking the train?* _____ B Yes, I am. I'm visiting my friend.

2 A _____ B No, I'm not. She's here.

3 A _____ B No, I'm not. I'm on the train.

4 A _____ B I'm walking to the movie theater.

5 A _____ B I'm going to a party.

6 A _____ B No. My brother has my bike.

B **You are on a bus. People are talking on their cell phones. Write two conversations. Use the words in the box in exercise 3A.**

1 A _____

 B _____

2 A _____

 B _____

7.3 A NEW LIFE

1 FUNCTIONAL LANGUAGE: Asking how things are going

A **Put the phone conversation in the correct order.**

	Jesse	Really? Me, too.
1	**Jesse**	Hello.
	Jesse	Hey, Gustavo!
	Jesse	Not bad, thanks. How are you?
	Gustavo	How are you doing?
	Gustavo	Hi, Jesse. It's Gustavo.
	Gustavo	I'm fine. I'm doing my homework right now.

2 REAL WORLD STRATEGY: Reacting to news

A **Read the sentences. Check (✓) good news, bad news, or ordinary news. Write *Oh*, *Oh wow!*, or *Oh no*.**

		Good news	Bad news	Ordinary news	Reaction
1	I love my new job!				
2	I'm helping my son with his homework.				
3	My grandmother is 100 years old.				
4	There are no rooms at the hotel today.				
5	I have one brother and one sister.				
6	I'm 20 minutes late for class.				

3 FUNCTIONAL LANGUAGE AND REAL-WORLD STRATEGY

A   **Complete the conversation.**

Anna   ¹_____Hello._____

Paul   Hi, Anna. ²_____ Paul.

Anna   ³_____, Paul. How ⁴_____ you?

Paul   Good. How are you ⁵_____?

Anna   ⁶_____ fine, thanks. Are you at home?

Paul   No. I'm driving to work.

Anna   On Sunday?

Paul   Yeah. I'm working on Sundays these days.

Anna   Oh, ⁷_____! Why?

Paul   I have a new job on weekends.

Anna   ⁸_____. Do you like it?

Paul   Yeah, I love it!

Anna   Oh, ⁹_____! That's great.

B   **Read about Sylvia and Rafael. How many children does Sylvia have? What is Rafael's bad news?**

Sylvia and Rafael are cousins. They live in Florida. Sylvia's children are six, nine, and fourteen years old. Sylvia is always busy – at work and at home. Rafael has some bad news. His wife, Pearl, is not in Florida right now. She is working in California.

C   **Sylvia and Rafael are talking. Write their conversation. Use the information in exercise 3B.**

_____   _____
_____   _____
_____   _____
_____   _____
_____   _____

7.4 CHAOS!

1 READING

A **SCAN** **Read the blog. When does the restaurant close?**

The Life of a Chef: A to Z by Chef Andy
B is for Busy!

[Thursday, January 15, 5:30 a.m.] I'm having breakfast at the restaurant. This is my favorite time of the day. There are no people here.

[Thursday, January 15, 6:00 a.m.] Now there are ten people in the restaurant. They're drinking coffee and chatting. The same ten people come every day from 6:00 to 7:00. Then they take the 7:10 train to work.

[Thursday, January 15, 8:30 a.m.] Here are the moms and dads with small children. They're walking to the restaurant. Now they're opening the door. Oh, no! The children are running in the restaurant. I don't like that.

[Thursday, January 15, 9:15 a.m.] I'm cooking today's lunch. The restaurant's servers, Nick and Alicia are helping me in the kitchen.

[Thursday, January 15, 11:15 a.m.] I'm eating lunch with Nick and Alicia. We always eat before people come for lunch.

[Thursday, January 15, 12:00 p.m.] It's noon now. People are waiting at the door. There are 20 people!

[Thursday, January 15, 2:30 p.m.] There usually aren't a lot of people in the restaurant in the afternoon. We're cleaning the kitchen and the tables in the dining area.

[Thursday, January 15, 4:30 p.m.] I'm cooking dinner. Mac and Pilar are helping me now. We are cooking food for 50 people! The restaurant closes at 11 p.m. It's a very busy day. But people love my food, so I love my job!

B **READ FOR DETAILS** **Read the blog again. Then complete the chart with the times.**

5:30 a.m.	Andy is having breakfast.		Andy is cooking lunch.
	Ten people are drinking coffee and talking.		Andy and two people are having lunch.
	Parents are coming to the restaurant with their children.		People are coming for lunch at the restaurant.
			Andy is cooking dinner.

2 LISTENING

A 🔊 **7.01** **LISTEN FOR SUPPORTING DETAILS** **Listen to Andy talk about his job. Choose the correct answers.**

1 How many people does Andy cook for every day?

 a 100 **b** four **c** 200

2 How many days a week is the restaurant open?

 a seven **b** three **c** four

3 Why do the people like the restaurant?

 a because they're not cooking at home **b** because the restaurant is busy

 c because they're not at work

4 What does Andy do in his free time?

 a cooks at home **b** eats in restaurants **c** helps his friends

3 **WRITING**

A   **Match 1–6 with a–f. Then write sentences below. Add _too_ or _also_ and use the correct punctuation.**

1   I like Nick and Alicia.   f   **a**   I cook dinner.   (too)
2   My job is busy.   **b**   They're playing with things.   (also)
3   The children are running in the restaurant.   ____   **c**   I'm a writer.   (too)
4   I cook breakfast and lunch.   ____   **d**   They come for dinner.   (also)
5   Mr and Mrs Garcia come for breakfast on Friday. ____   **e**   I work a lot of hours.   (also)
6   I'm a chef.   ____   **f**   I like Mac and Pilar.   (too)

1   _I like Nick and Alicia. I like Mac and Pilar, too._
2   _____
3   _____
4   _____
5   _____
6   _____

B   **Add _And, But_, or _Also_ to the sentences below. Use the correct punctuation.**

1   I like the blog.   ____And OR Also,____   I think the comments are interesting.
2   The writer has a busy life. _____ he has fun.
3   She works in a Mexican restaurant. _____ she goes to school at night.
4   Clara and Hugo really like the Couch Café. _____ they think it's expensive.

C   **Write a blog post about a day in your life. Give your blog a title (for example, _F is for Fun_). Write about what you do at different times of the day. What is your favorite time of the day? Why?**

CHECK AND REVIEW

Read the statements. Can you do these things?

UNIT 7	Mark the boxes. ☑ I can do it. ？ I am not sure. I can …	If you are not sure, go back to these pages in the Student's Book.
VOCABULARY	☐ use words about activities around the house. ☐ use transportation words.	page 66 page 68
GRAMMAR	☐ use the present continuous in statements. ☐ ask questions in the present continuous.	page 67 page 69
FUNCTIONAL LANGUAGE	☐ start a phone call. ☐ react to news.	page 70 page 71
SKILLS	☐ write a blog about things happening now. ☐ use _and, but_, and _also_.	page 73 page 73

8.1   SHE LIKES MUSIC, BUT SHE CAN'T DANCE!

1   VOCABULARY: Verbs to describe skills

A   **Look at the pictures and complete the sentences. Use the correct form of the verbs in the box.**

dance	draw	fix things	paint	play the guitar	read music
sing	skateboard	surf	snowboard	speak two languages	~~swim~~

1 Matt _____swims_____ every week.

2 Jorge is an artist and _____ beautiful pictures.

3 Sidney _____ for people.

4 Natalia is Mexican-American. She _____ _____.

5 Renato goes to the beach every weekend and _____.

6 Ben is in a music class and _____ well.

7 Jaime _____ in the mountains in winter.

8 Aiko often goes to the park and _____.

9 Lorena _____ in a band.

10 Paola _____ with her cousin at family parties.

11 Sergei _____ his favorite music in the morning.

12 Emma _____ with her friends after school.

58

2 GRAMMAR: *can* and *can't* for ability; *well*

A **Read the text. (Circle) *can* or *can't* to complete the sentences.**

My family is from the United States. My brother and I ¹(can)/ *can't* speak English and Spanish. My brother lives in France now, and he ²*can* / *can't* speak French, too. My mom only speaks English – she ³*can* / *can't* speak other languages. My dad ⁴*can* / *can't* speak other languages, but he ⁵*can* / *can't* read music. He loves his piano!

We have other skills, too. My mom ⁶*can* / *can't* fix things, for example the car, or our bikes. They always work well. My brother ⁷*can* / *can't* draw well, and he ⁸*can* / *can't* paint well, too. I love his pictures! I ⁹*can* / *can't* sing well – my brother says I'm not very good. But I ¹⁰*can* / *can't* dance – I love it!

B **Write sentences with *can*. Use the verbs in the box and *well*.**

| cook   draw   drive   play music   ~~play soccer~~   speak English |

1 Soccer players *can play soccer well.* _____
2 Bus drivers _____.
3 A chef _____.
4 English teachers _____.
5 An artist _____.
6 People in a band _____.

3 GRAMMAR AND VOCABULARY

A **Complete the chart for you. Then write questions and answers with *can* or *can't* and the words in parentheses ( ).**

	dance	draw	fix things	paint	play the guitar	read music	ride a bike	sing	skateboard	snowboard	speak two languages	surf	swim
Carla	✔	✗	✔	✗	✔	✔	✔	✔	✗	✗	✔	✗	✔
Tony	✔	✔	✔	✔	✗	✗	✔	✗	✔	✗	✔	✔	✔
You													

1 (Carla / play the guitar)   *Can Carla play the guitar? Yes, she can.* _____
2 (Tony / sing)   _____
3 (Carla and Tony / snowboard)   _____
4 (Carla and Tony / speak two languages) _____
5 (Carla / surf)   _____
6 (Tony / paint)   _____
7 (you / read music)   _____
8 (you / fix things)   _____

B **Look at the answers. Write questions about people you know. Use the verbs in exercise 3A.**

1 *Can your mother swim?* _____ Yes, she can.   4 _____ No, she can't.
2 _____ Yes, he can.   5 _____ No, they can't.
3 _____ No, he can't.   6 _____ Yes, they can.

8.2 HAPPY WORKERS = GREAT WORKERS?

1 VOCABULARY: Work

A **Complete the sentences with the words in the box.**

> company   coworkers   have a meeting   office
> take a break   think   work hard   workers

I work for a big ¹ _____company_____ . Its name is Verulia. There are 250 ² _____ in my company. Some people work in the capital city, but 50 of us work in Gardon, near my home. I like my ³ _____ . They are very friendly. The ⁴ _____ is nice because it is near a park. I usually ⁵ _____ at 10:30 for half an hour. I go for a walk in the park. Sometimes 10 or 15 of us ⁶ _____ in the park. It's really good because we ⁷ _____ of great ideas outside. I ⁸ _____ – sometimes for six days a week – but I love my job!

2 GRAMMAR: *can* and *can't* for possibility

A **Complete the sentences with *can* or *can't*.**

1 It's possible to swim in the lake.
   We ~~can swim in the lake.~~ _____

2 It's not possible to surf there.
   You _____

3 It's not possible to use my cell phone in the mountains.
   I _____

4 It's possible to ride our bikes in the park.
   We _____

5 Maria doesn't walk a lot. It's possible to take the bus.
   She _____

6 It's not possible for a dog to go in a restaurant.
   A dog _____

60

B **Write questions about your English class.**
Use *can* or *can't* and the words in parentheses ( ).
Then write answers for the questions.

1 (be late for class)

  Can you be late for class?

  No, I (OR we) can't.

2 (speak your language in class)

  _____

  _____

3 (ask your teacher questions)

  _____

  _____

4 (use your cell phone in class)

  _____

  _____

5 (when / have a meeting with your teacher)

  _____

  _____

6 (what / do on your break)

  _____

  _____

3 GRAMMAR AND VOCABULARY

A **Look at the chart. How are New Tech Company and Best Tech Company different? Write sentences about each company. Use *can* and *can't*.**

	New Tech Company	Best Tech Company
work at home or in the office	✔	
work in the office every day		✔
30 hours a week + 10 minute coffee break every day		✔
50 hours a week + breaks when you want	✔	
meetings in the office three times a week		✔
Skype meetings every month	✔	

1 *At New Tech Company, you can work from home or in the office.*

2 _____

3 _____

4 _____

B **Do you want to work at New Tech Company or Best Tech Company? Write your answer.**
Give two or three reasons.

_____

_____

_____

1   FUNCTIONAL LANGUAGE: Giving and asking for opinions

A   **Put the words into the correct order to make questions.**

1   Do / have happy workers?/ that / you / think / great companies

    Do you think that great companies have happy workers?

2   Why / friends are important? / you / do / think

    _____

3   you / technology / a good thing? / is / think / Do

    _____

4   fun? / you / think / Do / school / is

    _____

5   a job? / Why / you / think / want / do / people

    _____

B   **Match the questions from exercise 1A with the answers below.**

a   _____   Yes. I think technology is changing the world. It's good.

b   _____   I think people want a job because they want money.

c   _____   Yes, I do. I think that good companies always have happy workers.

d   _____   No. I think school is boring.

e   _____   I think friends are important because they are fun and interesting.

C   **Answer the questions so they are true for you. Give your opinion. Use *I think so* or *I don't think so*.**

1   Are you good at sports?   *I don't think so.*

2   Are you a good worker?   _____

3   Are you good at video games?   _____

4   Are you a good coworker?   _____

5   Are you good at teamwork?   _____

2   REAL-WORLD STRATEGY: Explaining and saying more about an idea

A   **Circle *a* or *b* to complete the sentences.**

1   I think this is a great company. I mean,

    (a) It's a good place to work.

    b I'm a really good worker.

2   We love our dog. I mean,

    a her name is Kiki.

    b she's always fun and happy.

3   My coworkers are great. I mean,

    a we work well together.

    b we work in the same office.

4   I'm not very good at soccer. I mean,

    a I watch soccer on TV, but I can't *play* soccer.

    b I watch soccer with my friends a lot.

FUNCTIONAL LANGUAGE AND REAL-WORLD STRATEGY

A   **Bill has an interview for a job at a restaurant. Use the expressions in the box to complete the conversation.**

> Do you think that …   I don't think so.   I mean, …   I think so.

Chef Are you the right person for this job?

Bill Yeah. ¹_____

Chef Why are you a good server?

Bill Because on weekends, I go to different restaurants with my friends, and I see a lot of servers. The good servers are friendly. I'm friendly, too.

Chef OK. ²_____ it's important to work well with other servers?

Bill ³_____. I mean, servers don't work with other servers.

Chef Really? In my restaurant, teamwork is important. The servers work with the chefs in the kitchen.

Bill Oh.

Chef Our busy days are Friday, Saturday, and Sunday. Can you work then?

Bill I can't work on Saturday and Sunday. ⁴_____ I'm busy on weekends. But I can work on Tuesday, Wednesday, and Thursday.

B   **Is Bill is the right person for the job? Why or why not?**

_____

_____

C   **Write a conversation between the chef and a woman, Sofia. The chef thinks Sofia is the right person for the job.**

_____

_____

_____

_____

_____

_____

_____

_____

_____

_____

_____

_____

_____

COMPUTERS AND OUR JOBS

1 LISTENING

A 🔊 **8.01** **LISTEN FOR DETAILS** **Listen to part of a podcast about robots. What do Emily and Joel think?** (Circle) **the correct answer.**

Emily and Joel *think / do not think* that a robot can be a child's friend.

B 🔊 **8.01** **LISTEN FOR SUPPORTING DETAILS** **Listen again. What is good about robots for children? Check (✓) the things Emily and Joel say.**

1 Children can play games with robots.   ☐
2 Children can learn about technology from robots.   ☐
3 Children can play soccer with robots.   ☐
4 Robots and children can have birthday parties.   ☐
5 Robots are not real friends.   ☐
6 Children can do things with robots all day.   ☐

2 READING

A **Read the article. Then choose the correct title.** (Circle) **1, 2, or 3.**

1 New Robots
2 Our Grandparents' Problems
3 Robots for Our Grandparents

Companies now have talking robots for grandparents. Sometimes, our grandparents do not live with other people. They do not talk to other people every day and they don't see their friends often. This is a problem, and the new robots can help.

Elena Cho is an example. She is an old woman. She doesn't live with her family. But now, she has a talking robot. It can tell her about new books or interesting movies. Also, it can play music for Elena. Her robot knows her favorite songs and singers.

Elena Cho says, "My robot is not a friend, but I like it very much."

B **Read the article again. Check (✓) the correct sentences.**

1 Some grandparents do not live with other people.   ✔
2 New robots can help grandparents.   _____
3 Elena Cho's robot goes to the movies with her.   _____
4 Elena Cho's robot plays her favorite music.   _____
5 Elena doesn't like her robot.   _____

3 WRITING

A **Read three people's online comments about the podcast. Find the quotes from Emily and Joel. Change the punctuation for the quotes.**

Claudia, Bogotá
I don't think Emily is right. She says our children are playing with their robots and not with other children. My two children often play with other children. They use robots for 30 minutes a day. I don't think that's a lot.

Helena, Belo Horizonte
I think robots are a good thing. Joel says children can play with robots and learn from them. I agree. Children can play with other children, but I don't think they learn from other children. They learn from their robots.

Moe, Toronto
I think Emily is right. Robots are sometimes a problem for children. She says robots are now our children's friends. It's true for my six-year-old nephew. He always plays with his robot. He doesn't want to play with other children. It's a big problem for my sister and her husband.

B **Look at the sentences about robots for old people. Change the sentences to quotes. Use *says* or *said* and the correct punctuation.**

Informal writing:

1 Elena Cho: I like my new talking robot.

2 Elena Cho's son: The robot helps my mother a lot.

Formal writing:

3 Ronaldo Benson: Our company makes robots for grandparents.

4 Doctor Wu: Robots are good for grandparents because their families don't see them every day.

C **Write an online comment. Give your opinion about robots for grandparents.**

CHECK AND REVIEW

Read the statements. Can you do these things?

UNIT 8	Mark the boxes. ☑ I can do it. ? I am not sure.	If you are not sure, go back to these pages in the Student's Book.
	I can …	
VOCABULARY	☐ use verbs to describe skills.	page 76
	☐ use words about work.	page 78
GRAMMAR	☐ use *can* or *can't* for ability.	page 77
	☐ use *well*.	page 77
	☐ use *can* or *can't* for possibility.	page 79
FUNCTIONAL LANGUAGE	☐ ask for and give opinions.	page 80
	☐ explain and say more about an idea.	page 81
SKILLS	☐ write an online comment.	page 83
	☐ use quotations for other people's words.	page 83

UNIT 9 PLACES TO GO

9.1 I LOVE IT HERE!

1 VOCABULARY: Travel

A **Complete the sentences with the words in the box.**

boat	country	plane	ranch
tickets	tour	town	~~vacation~~

1 Silvia and Raúl aren't working. They are on _____vacation_____ .

2 Raúl loves animals. He's on a farm in the _____ , away from the city.

3 Silvia loves the ocean. She goes on a _____ on the water.

4 Silvia and Raúl buy _____ for the museum. They are $25 each.

5 Silvia doesn't like animals. A _____ is not a good place for her.

6 Silvia lives in a small _____ . It has 10,000 people.

7 Silvia and Raúl go on a _____ of the museum. A woman tells them about the interesting art.

8 Silvia sits next to Raúl on the _____ . She looks out the window and sees buildings and trees.

2 GRAMMAR: *This* and *These*

A **Complete the conversations. Use *this* or *these* and the words in the box.**

museum	photos	seats
your hotel	your tickets	~~your train~~

1 A Is _____this your train_____ ?

   B Yes, it is. We're going home.

2 A Are _____ ?

   B Yes. We need them for the movie.

3 A _____ cool.

   B Yes. They are from our vacation.

4 A Is _____ ?

   B Yes, our room is very nice!

5 A Wow, _____ comfortable.

   B Yes, they are.

6 A _____ interesting.

   B Yes. It has a lot of beautiful pictures.

66

3 GRAMMAR AND VOCABULARY

A Look at the pictures from people's vacations. Imagine you are writing messages about each trip. Write two or three sentences for each picture. Use *this* or *these*. How many words from the box can you use?

boat	country	farm	ranch	plane	ticket	tour	town	vacation

1 We're on a bike tour. There are many interesting places on the tour. It's not boring!

2

3

9.2 SAN FRANCISCO, HERE WE COME

1 VOCABULARY: Travel arrangements

A **Cross out the words that do <u>not</u> complete the sentences.**

1	We have to arrive _____ at 2 p.m.	at our destination	at the airport	~~on a trip~~
2	They are buying _____.	friends	some coffee	tickets
3	The flight _____ at 10 a.m.	arrives	leaves	stays
4	We are _____ my aunt's house.	checking in at	staying at	traveling to
5	Our _____ is from June 15 to July 1.	destination	trip	vacation
6	We can check in at the _____.	airport	hotel	museum
7	We _____ on the plane for 12 hours.	arrive	fly	travel
8	People can buy plane tickets _____.	at the airport	online	on a flight

2 GRAMMAR: *like to, want to, need to, have to*

A (Circle) the correct answers.

1 My husband has a business trip this week. He (*has to*) / *likes to* go to Boston.

2 This is our favorite restaurant. We *like to* / *need to* go there for lunch on Sunday.

3 My brother is studying to be a doctor. He *wants to* / *needs to* study for five years.

4 This camera is not in the stores. You *want to* / *have to* buy it online.

5 Can we take the bus to the mall? I don't *have to* / *want to* drive.

6 My friends and I are learning Chinese. *We want to* / *need to* go to China on vacation next year.

7 I *like to* / *have to* eat cookies for breakfast, but I know it's bad for me.

8 My friend *wants to* / *likes to* work at a big technology company. She has an interview there next week!

B   **Complete the sentences with affirmative (+) or negative (–) forms of *have to*, *like to*, *need to*, or *want to*. Sometimes there are two correct answers.**

1   It's 10 a.m. My flight is at 12 p.m. I'm late! I ____need to__ OR __have to___ go to the airport.

2   My sister _____ go on vacation with our parents. She likes to travel with her friends.

3   Jason's very hungry. He _____ eat dinner now.

4   Sari _____ travel on the subway. It's busy and hot.

5   My parents' car is very old. They _____ buy a new car.

6   We're planning our next vacation. We _____ go to a lot of interesting places.

3   GRAMMAR AND VOCABULARY

A   **Write sentences that are true for you.**

1   have / check in / three hours before my flight

  I have to check in three hours before my flight at the airport near my city.

2   like / fly

  _____

3   have / buy plane tickets online

  _____

4   like / stay at hotels

  _____

5   need / arrive / at the bus stop 15 minutes early

  _____

6   want / work / at an airport

  _____

7   need / leave / home before 8:00 a.m.

  _____

8   like / take / trips to places near my home

  _____

9   want / travel / to New York

  _____

THEY'RE TWO FOR $15

1 FUNCTIONAL LANGUAGE: Asking for missing information and clarification

A **Correct <u>four</u> mistakes in the conversations.**

1 A Excuse me. Where ^is the women's restroom?
   B It's over there, near the door.

2 A Excuse me. What time the bus to San Diego leave?
   B It leaves at 11:15 a.m.

3 A Excuse me. How much this guide book?
   B It's $12.99.

4 A Excuse me. I need buy a ticket to Bogotá. How much is it?
   B A bus ticket $147.

B **Put the conversation in the correct order.**

_____ A And for a child? Is it the same price?

__1__ A Excuse me. How much is one ticket?

_____ A Then one ticket for me and one ticket for my son, please.

_____ A Where are seats 10A and 10B?

_____ B Tickets are $15.

__8__ B They're on the right.

_____ B OK. Your seats are 10A and 10B.

_____ B No, it isn't. Tickets for children are $5.

2 REAL-WORLD STRATEGY: Asking someone to repeat something

A **Check (✓) <u>two</u> correct ways to ask someone to repeat something.**

1 Sorry, repeat, please. _____

2 Sorry, can you repeat that, please? _____

3 Sorry, what you say? _____

4 Sorry, can you say that again? _____

3 FUNCTIONAL LANGUAGE AND REAL-WORLD STRATEGY

A   **Mia is at a store. She talks to a clerk. Use the information below to write their conversation.**

1 Mia wants to know the price of the flowers.
2 The clerk says a price.
3 Mia wants to know the price of a plant, too.
4 The clerk says a price for the flowers and the plant together.
5 Mia doesn't understand.
6 The clerk repeats the information.

7 Mia understands. Now she wants to know where a good café is.
8 The clerk gives directions.
9 Mia doesn't understand.
10 The clerk repeats the directions.
11 Mia thanks the clerk.
12 The clerk finishes the conversation.

1 **Mia**   Excuse me. How much are the flowers?
2 **Clerk**
3 **Mia**
4 **Clerk**
5 **Mia**
6 **Clerk**
7 **Mia**
8 **Clerk**
9 **Mia**
10 **Clerk**
11 **Mia**
12 **Clerk**

1 READING

A   **SKIM** **Skim the article. Check (✓) the things the article mentions.**

☐ horses   ☐ museums   ☐ hotels

☐ countries in South America   ☐ food

South American ranch vacations ✈

**Do you like animals and nature? Do you want to travel and meet people?
Why not visit a *gaucho* ranch?**

A *gaucho* ranch is a very big farm with horses and other animals. The workers there are called *gauchos*. They are really good with horses. People can visit *gaucho* ranches and learn about the farm and the animals.

Can you ride a horse well? The *gauchos* can take you on a tour of the ranch.

Do you want to learn to ride a horse? The *gauchos* can help you!

There are *gaucho* ranches in South America, for example in Argentina, Bolivia, Chile, and Uruguay. You can visit for a week, or you can work on a *gaucho* ranch for a month. Some ranches even have one-day tours.

You don't have to ride a horse every day. You can also walk around the ranch and see all the interesting plants and animals.

Maybe you don't want to go to the country, but you're interested in ranches. Some towns near ranches have *gaucho* museums. One *gaucho* museum is only 90 minutes from Buenos Aires. You can go there and learn a lot about *gaucho* life. Also, the museum is free!

So, go to a *gaucho* ranch and have a great vacation!

An Argentinian *gaucho* on his horse

B   **Read the article again. Answer the questions. Write complete sentences.**

1 Where does a gaucho work?

2 What countries have gaucho ranches?

3 How long can you stay at a gaucho ranch?

4 What can you learn about in a gaucho museum?

2 LISTENING

A   🔊 **9.01** **LISTEN FOR DETAILS** **Listen to Ella talk about her vacation. Does she like it?**

B   🔊 **9.01** **LISTEN FOR SUPPORTING DETAILS** **Listen again. Choose the correct answer.**

1 Ella is visiting _____.

   a a ranch   **b** an island   **c** a museum

2 What does Ella think about the people there?

   a They are interesting.   **b** They are different.   **c** They are friendly.

3 What can Ella do in the afternoon?

   a cook lunch   **b** go for a walk   **c** talk to her mother

4 Next year, Ella wants to _____.

   a come with her mother **b** stay longer   **c** get a bigger room

WRITING

A   **Read the advice below. Complete the paragraphs with affirmative (+) and negative (–) imperative verbs in the box.**

> drive   eat   go x2   ~~read~~   ride   take

How to plan your ranch vacation

Ranch vacations in Argentina are great, but [1] _____read_____ the online reviews before you go.
[2] _____ from October to December or from April to June. These are good times to visit.
[3] _____ from January to March. It can be very hot. Some ranches are hundreds of miles from Buenos Aires. [4] _____ to the ranches in a car. It's very far. [5] _____ a plane and then a taxi.

Is this your first time on a horse? You can have lessons on the ranch. They're not expensive. Or can you ride a horse well? [6] _____ to a different part of the ranch every day. Ranches are really big. You need to visit for a week or two!

[7] _____ a lot at lunch. Dinner is a big meal, and the food is great!

B   **Change the formal sentences to informal sentences. Use imperatives.**

1   You need to come for a week.   _Come for a week._
2   You can visit the place in August.   _____
3   You have to take a taxi.   _____
4   You need to eat a big breakfast   _____

C   **Think about a place you like. Write about what people can do and see there. Use imperatives to give advice.**

CHECK AND REVIEW

Read the statements. Can you do these things?

UNIT 9	Mark the boxes. ✔ I can do it. ? I am not sure.		If you are not sure, go back to these pages in the Student's Book.
	I can …		
VOCABULARY	☐ use travel words.		page 86
	☐ use words for travel arrangements.		page 88
GRAMMAR	☐ use *this* and *these*.		page 87
	☐ use *like to, want to, have to,* and *need to.*		page 89
FUNCTIONAL LANGUAGE	☐ ask for and give missing information.		page 90
	☐ ask someone to repeat something.		page 91
SKILLS	☐ write a description of a place.		page 93
	☐ use imperatives to give advice.		page 93

WHITE NIGHTS

1 VOCABULARY: Going out

A **Use the words in the box to complete the conversation.**

| eat | get | go | have | look at | meet | take x2 |

A What do you usually do on the weekend? I need ideas!

B I visit the mall and ¹_____ shopping. Sometimes I ²_____ together with friends. What about you?

A I like to go to the museum near my home and ³_____ art. I like to ⁴_____ a walk outside, too. I often go to the park.

B The park is great! You can ⁵_____ a picnic in the park. It's fun to ⁶_____ outside!

A Good idea! I never have picnics in the park. Usually I ⁷_____ my husband out to dinner at our favorite restaurant. But not this weekend.

B Oh? Why not? Where is he?

A He's in New York right now. He's going to be home next week. I want to ⁸_____ him at the airport.

2 GRAMMAR: Statements with *be going to*

A **Imagine that it is 10 a.m. on Thursday, July 6. Look at the future plans below. Replace the <u>underlined</u> words with future time expressions from the box. You won't use all the words.**

next month	on Saturday	this weekend	next Saturday	this afternoon
this year	next week	this month	tomorrow	next weekend
this Saturday	tonight	next year	this week	

1 I'm going to swim <u>in six hours</u>.

    I'm going to swim this afternoon.

2 The doctor is going to call <u>in 24 hours</u>.

    _____

3 Miriam is going to have a party <u>on August 6</u>.

    _____

4 We're going to meet our friend <u>in two days</u>.

    _____

5 We're going to buy the tickets <u>in 10 hours</u>.

    _____

6 They aren't going to have a picnic <u>in seven days</u>.

    _____

B **Write sentences with *be going to*.**

1 It's Monday today. I meet my friends every Tuesday.

   I'm going to meet my friends tomorrow _____ .

2 Felipe takes a walk every night.

   _____ tonight.

3 Marco and his friends go to the mall every weekend.

   _____ next weekend.

4 Sara doesn't want to take a trip next year.

   _____ next year.

5 Kate and her coworkers take a break every day at 11:00.

   _____ this morning at 11:00.

6 I have class every Tuesday.

   _____ on Tuesday.

3 GRAMMAR AND VOCABULARY

A **Look at Simon's plans for Friday, Saturday, and Sunday. Write sentences about what he is going to do.**

Thursday	Friday	Saturday	Sunday
Today!	Meet my friend at the airport	Picnic at the beach	Go shopping at the mall
	Take my friend out for dinner		Free time

1 *On Friday, Simon is going to meet his friend at the airport.*

2 _____

3 _____

4 _____

5 _____

B **Write five true sentences about you. Use the words in exercise 1A, *be going to*, and future time expressions from exercise 2A.**

1 *I'm going to meet my sister tomorrow afternoon. Then we're going to go shopping.*

2 _____

3 _____

4 _____

5 _____

6 _____

10.2 BUT IT'S SUMMER THERE!

1 VOCABULARY: Clothes; seasons

A **Cross out the word that does <u>not</u> belong in each sentence.**

1 jeans   pants   ~~T-shirt~~   4 shorts   sweater   skirt

2 shorts   coat   hat   5 sweater   shirt   boots

3 dress   shoes   boots   6 pants   skirt   jeans

B **Read the descriptions of clothes. Which season is each person talking about? Write words in the box.**

dry season	fall	rainy season	spring	summer	winter

1 There's no rain, and it's hot! I wear shorts every day. _____dry season_____

2 It's very cold! I'm wearing a coat and a hat. _____

3 I'm on the beach. I'm wearing shorts and a T-shirt, and no shoes! _____

4 It's not summer, but I can see new flowers. I'm wearing a shirt and pants. I don't need to wear a sweater. _____

5 There's a lot of rain, but it's not cold. I'm wearing a coat and my big boots. _____

6 I'm wearing a dress. I have a coat, but I'm not wearing it. The next season is winter. _____

2 GRAMMAR: Questions with *be going to*

A **Read the sentences and complete the questions. Then answer the questions so they are true for you. Write short answers.**

1 I'm not going to get together with friends this weekend.

Are you going to get together _____ with friends next weekend?

_____ Yes, I am. OR No, I'm not. _____

2 My friend isn't going to meet me tonight.

_____ you tomorrow?

_____

3 My family and I aren't going to be on vacation this month.

_____ next month?

_____

4 My friends aren't going to take me out to dinner this week.

_____ you out to dinner next week?

_____

5 My teacher isn't going to work this summer.

_____ next summer?

_____

6 I'm not going to buy a car in the spring.

_____ next fall?

B **Write questions for the answers. Use *What, When, Where,* or *Who*.**

1 A *Who are you going to meet?*

   B I'm going to meet my cousins.

2 A _____

   B The class is going to take a break in 20 minutes.

3 A _____

   B The stores are going to open at 9 a.m.

4 A _____

   B We're going to go shopping at the mall.

5 A _____

   B My brother is going to buy a TV.

6 A _____

   B I'm going to visit my parents.

3 GRAMMAR AND VOCABULARY

A **Use the words to write questions. Then write true answers. Use *be going to*.**

1 who / you / visit / this fall

   Who are you going to visit this fall?

   I'm going to visit my friend in Canada.

2 who / go / with / you / on your trip

_____

_____

3 what clothes / you / take / on your next trip

_____

_____

4 when / you / buy / boots

_____

_____

5 what / country / you / travel / in the rainy season?

_____

_____

6 where / your friend / wear / her new dress

_____

_____

7 where / your cousin / buy / new pants

_____

_____

8 when / you / wear / a sweater

_____

_____

LET'S MEET AT THE HOTEL

1 FUNCTIONAL LANGUAGE: Making and responding to suggestions

A **Look at the conversations. Circle the correct responses.**

1 **A** There's a good Chinese restaurant near here.

    B **a** Why don't we eat Chinese food?

        (b) Why don't we walk there?

2 **A** I don't want to cook dinner tonight.

    B **a** Let's eat at home.

        b Let's go to a restaurant.

3 **A** It's a beautiful day outside.

    B **a** Why don't we take a walk?

        b Why don't we watch a movie?

4 **A** The museum is 15 kilometers from here.

    B **a** Let's walk to the museum.

        b Let's take a bus.

5 **A** Let's eat outside.

    B **a** Yes, we do.

        b Good idea.

6 **A** Why don't we have a picnic on Sunday?

    B **a** Sorry, I'm busy.

        b No, we don't.

7 **A** Why don't we meet at the hotel?

    B **a** Yes, sure.

        b Let's meet at the hotel.

8 **A** Let's go to the beach.

    B **a** I'm sorry.

        b OK, sounds good.

2 REAL-WORLD STRATEGY: Saying why you can't do something

A **Look at Amy's week below. Then write her responses to sentences 1–5. Use *have to*.**

> *Things to do next week:*
>
> **Monday — Friday** — work from 8 a.m.–4 p.m.
>
> **Monday** — doctor, 6 p.m.
>
> **Tuesday** — make dinner for my family
>
> **Saturday** — Aunt Beatriz's party
>
> **Sunday** — study

1 Let's go to the mall Monday evening.   **Amy**   *I'm sorry, but I can't. I have to go to the doctor.*

2 Why don't we meet for lunch on Friday?   **Amy** _____

3 Let's have dinner together on Tuesday.   **Amy** _____

4 Why don't we get together on Saturday?   **Amy** _____

5 Let's go to the beach on Sunday.   **Amy** _____

3 FUNCTIONAL LANGUAGE AND REAL-WORLD STRATEGY

A **Alex and Jay are making plans for their friend Keiko's birthday. Put the sentences in the correct order.**

_____	**Keiko**	Hello.
_____	**Alex**	Good idea. Let's go to the new Korean restaurant on First Street. It's really good.
1	**Alex**	So, it's Keiko's birthday on Friday.
_____	**Keiko**	I'm sorry, but I can't. I'm busy then. My family is going to have a birthday party for me. Hey, why don't you and Alex come to the party?
_____	**Alex**	Hi, Keiko. It's Alex. Jay and I are talking about your birthday. We want to take you out for dinner. Why don't we meet at the new Korean restaurant next Friday?
_____	**Jay**	OK, great. Let's call Keiko and ask her.
_____	**Jay**	Oh, yeah! Why don't we take her out to dinner for her birthday?
9	**Alex**	Thanks, Keiko. We love birthday parties. We can take you out to dinner next weekend.
_____	**Alex**	Sure. I have her number on my phone. I'm calling her now …

B **Read the information below. Then write a conversation.**

You are making plans with two friends for next weekend. Talk about what you are going to do and when you are going to do it. You and your friends are not free at the same time. Find a time to get together.

_____

_____

_____

_____

_____

_____

_____

_____

_____

10.4 A 24-HOUR CITY

1 LISTENING

A 🔊 **10.01** **LISTEN FOR DETAILS** Listen to Susana talk about her trip to Stockholm, Sweden. Check (✓) the things Susana says about Stockholm.

☐ It's famous.

☐ There are old buildings.

☐ There are a lot of things to do.

☐ It's not hot.

B 🔊 **10.01** **LISTEN FOR SUPPORTING DETAILS** Listen again. Put the things to do in the order Susana says them. Cross out the sentences that she does not talk about.

_____ **a** go to a museum

_____ **b** go to the beach

_____ **c** go to an island

_____ **d** find a place to go dancing

_____ **e** go shopping and eat something

_____ **f** go for a bike ride

1 **g** tour famous places

_____ **h** have a picnic

2 READING

A Read the article about Midsummer Day in Sweden. Write *T* if the sentence is true or *F* if the sentence is false.

Midsummer Day is a very important day in Sweden. There is sun in the day *and* night. The holiday is on June 24, but the activities are always on the weekend. People wear holiday clothes for the day's activities, and they wear flowers, too. Children and adults dance and play games. They eat different foods – and the first strawberries of summer. Midsummer is also a time of love. Girls and young women take home seven different flowers. When they go to sleep on Midsummer Night, they see who their husband is going to be. Midsummer Day is really an important day.

strawberries

Midsummer Day in Sweden

T **1** It is always in June.

_____ **2** Midsummer Day is only for children.

_____ **3** People wear different clothes.

_____ **4** Flowers are important.

3 WRITING

A   Read the online invitation. <u>Underline</u> <u>six</u> full forms. Change the full forms to contractions.

Event   Beach party!
Host   Brianna
When?   Saturday, June 20
Where? Miami Beach

Message from Brianna

<u>Jeff is</u> going to be 25 on June 10. We are going to have a beach party for him. Be at Miami Beach near Fifth Street at 6:00 p.m. We are going to have a big picnic. Then we are going to go out. It is going to be a fun night! Do not tell Jeff about the party. He does not know about it.

Jeff's

B   Circle the contractions in the sentences. Write *F* if the sentence is formal. Write *I* if the sentence is informal.

1   There's going to be dancing.   I

2   Jenny is going to send the invitation.   _____

3   I am going to ask 30 people to come to the party.   _____

4   We're going to have a lot of fun.   _____

5   Do not be late.   _____

C   Imagine it's a friend's birthday party. Write an invitation for their party. Describe what you are going to do. Use contractions.

CHECK AND REVIEW

Read the statements. Can you do these things?

UNIT 10	Mark the boxes. ☑ I can do it. ? I am not sure. I can …	If you are not sure, go back to these pages in the Student's Book.
VOCABULARY	☐ use words for going out activities.	page 98
	☐ use words for clothes and seasons.	page 100
GRAMMAR	☐ use *be going to* in statements.	page 99
	☐ use *be going to* in *yes/no* and information questions.	page 101
FUNCTIONAL LANGUAGE	☐ make and respond to suggestions.	page 102
	☐ say why I can't do something.	page 103
SKILLS	☐ write an online invitation.	page 105
	☐ use contractions.	page 105

11.1   FLASHBACK FRIDAY

1 VOCABULARY: Describing people, places, and things

A **Match the adjectives (1–5) with their opposites (a–e).**

1 awful   _e_   a boring

2 exciting _____   b noisy

3 fast   _____   c old

4 new   _____   d slow

5 quiet   _____   e wonderful

B **Cross out the word that people do <u>not</u> use with *beautiful* and *cute*.**

1 **beautiful**   day   girl   man   picture   woman

2 **cute**   class   dog   dress   little boy   little girl

2 GRAMMAR: Statements with *was* and *were*

A **Complete the sentences with *was*, *wasn't*, *were*, or *weren't*.**

1 I'm tall now, but I _____wasn't_____ a tall child.

2 My grandparents are always home now, but in 2015, they _____ at work.

3 We're in the same class now, but we _____ in the same class last year.

4 Gabriel is in college now, but in 2016, he _____ in high school.

5 I'm not on vacation now, but I _____ on vacation last week.

6 School is fun now, but it _____ fun before.

7 Yessica is good at basketball now, but she _____ good last year.

8 You're here now, but you _____ here at 10 o'clock.

9 My friends are in college now, but they _____ last year.

10 Sergio _____ at our company last year, but now he is.

11 It _____ nice and quiet in my house this morning because my children _____ asleep.

12 I _____ in the office all week, but I'm not today because it's Sunday!

B   **Read the postcard. Then complete the sentences with** *was, wasn't, were,* **or** *weren't.*

July 10

Hi Leonor,

Tony and I are having a wonderful vacation.
We're at the beach right now. He's swimming,
and I'm writing this postcard! This beach is
beautiful, but it's noisy. There are a lot of
really cute children here, and they're playing
near us. But that's OK. It's a beautiful day,
and we're having a great time.
How are you?
Love,
Ines

1   It's August now. Ines _____ on vacation in July.

2   Ines's parents _____ with her.

3   Ines and Tony _____ at the beach on July 10.

4   The beach _____ quiet.

5   There _____ a lot of children.

3 GRAMMAR AND VOCABULARY

A   **Read the sentences. Then write two sentences that are the opposite. Use** *wasn't* **or** *weren't* **for A.**
     Use *was* **or** *were* **for B.**

1   I was quiet in class.

     A I wasn't quiet in class. _____   B I was noisy in class. _____

2   I was awful at sports in school.

     A _____   B _____

3   My school was in an old neighborhood.

     A _____   B _____

4   New books were boring for me.

     A _____   B _____

5   My first job was wonderful.

     A _____   B _____

6   My friends and I were noisy.

     A _____   B _____

7   My first computer was new.

     A _____   B _____

8   I was a good student.

     A _____   B _____

OUR OLD PHONE WAS GREEN

1 VOCABULARY: Colors

A **Unscramble the color words.**

1 ckbal _____

2 earong _____

3 twihe _____

4 dre _____

5 llowye _____

6 gary _____

7 lbeu _____

8 pkni _____

9 neerg _____

10 nrowb _____

11 lepurp _____

B **Complete the sentences so they are true for you. Use color words from exercise 1A.**

1 My cell phone is _____ .

2 My favorite shirt is _____ .

3 My bag is _____ .

4 I'm wearing _____ clothes today.

5 I don't like the color _____ .

2 GRAMMAR: Questions with *was* and *were*

A **Complete the *yes/no* questions with *was* or *were*. Then answer the questions so they are true for you. Use short answers.**

1 I wasn't at home on Sunday.

Were you at home on Saturday? _____   Yes, I was. OR No, I wasn't.

2 My family and I weren't on vacation in August.

_____ on vacation in June? _____

3 I wasn't in class on Tuesday.

_____ in class on Wednesday? _____

4 My cousins weren't in college in 2016.

_____ in college in 2017? _____

5 My friends weren't busy on Saturday.

_____ busy on Friday? _____

6 My teacher wasn't at work on Sunday.

_____ at work on Monday? _____

B **Use the words to write questions with *was* or *were*. Then answer the questions so they are true for you.**

1 what / your first teacher's name

What was your first teacher's name?   My first teacher's name was Ms. Song.

2 where / your first school

3 how old / you / in 2005

4 what color / your first cell phone

5 where / you / on Saturday night

6 who / with you / on the weekend

3 **GRAMMAR AND VOCABULARY**

A **Read the questions about when you were a child. Correct the mistake in each question. Then answer the questions so they are true for you.**

1 What things ~~was~~ brown in your home?
         were

Our kitchen table and chairs were brown.

2 What your favorite color was?

3 What color were your favorite toy?

4 Was your shoes always black?

5 Your desk was white?

6 Are there gray walls in your first home?

I HAVE NO IDEA

1 FUNCTIONAL LANGUAGE: Expressing uncertainty

A **Erica and Chris are at a party. Erica asks questions about the people she sees. Circle the correct words to complete the conversation.**

Erica Who's that man over there?

Chris ¹I'm *not* / *no* sure. ²I *think* / *know* he's Alma's brother.

Erica OK. And who's the woman next to him?

Chris Oh, that's Jamie's wife. Her name is Mischa, ³I *know* / *think*.

Erica Right. Where's Alma? It's her birthday party and I can't see her!

Chris ⁴I have *no* / *not* idea!

Erica There's Jamie. ⁵*Maybe* / *Yeah* Jamie can tell us!

2 REAL-WORLD STRATEGY: Taking time to think

A **Chris needs time to think about Erica's questions. Write *Let me think*, *Uh*, or *Um* in the conversation. There can sometimes be more than one answer.**

Erica Do you need more food, Chris?

Chris _____, I'm not hungry, thanks.

Erica What time do you want to leave?

Chris _____. Maybe in an hour?

Erica Do you want to dance?

Chris _____, yeah!

FUNCTIONAL LANGUAGE AND REAL-WORLD STRATEGY

A **Read sentences 1–5. Write a conversation between you and a friend. Use the words in the box in your friend's answers.**

I have no idea.	Uh, …	I don't know.	I think …
Maybe …	Um, …	Let me think.	I'm not sure.

1 You want to know Leonardo DiCaprio's age in *Titanic*.

    You   How old was Leonardo DiCaprio in *Titanic*?

Your friend   Uh, I don't know.

2 You want to know where Leonardo DiCaprio's parents are from.

    You

Your friend

3 You want to know the name of the actor in a TV show.

    You

Your friend

4 You want to know when a movie was popular.

    You

Your friend

5 You want to know who is in a famous band.

    You

Your friend

THINGS WE KEEP

1 READING

A SKIM **Read the article. Find <u>three</u> reasons why people keep things.**

Why do we keep things?

Old toys. Old music. Old soccer balls. Why are they so important? Why do we keep them? Here are three reasons:

Our feelings

5 Maybe your favorite toy when you were a child was from your grandparents. You don't play with the toy now. You never see it. But you still want to keep it. Why? Because it's from your grandparents. You love them very much. So you
10 keep the toy.

Money

Do you have your parents' old music? Maybe the music was five dollars in the 1970s. Maybe it is going to be 50 or 100 dollars in 20 years. Sometimes we keep things because we can get money for them in the future.

15 #### The future

Why are you keeping your old soccer ball or your old guitar? You don't need them now. You don't play soccer or the guitar. But maybe your son or daughter is going to be a great soccer player or a wonderful guitar player. You're keeping them for your children.

B READ FOR DETAIL **Read words 1–5 below. (Circle) the words in the article. Then match the words with their meanings (a–g). You don't need to use all the meanings.**

1 it (*line 7*)	_g_	**a** children	**f** things
2 them (*line 9*)	___	**b** grandparents	**g** toy
3 it (*line 13*)	___	**c** music	
4 them (*line 14*)	___	**d** parents	
5 them (*line 18*)	___	**e** soccer ball or guitar	

2 LISTENING

A 🔊 11.01 LISTEN FOR DETAILS **Listen to the conversation. Write *T* for True and *F* for False.**

___ **1** Tadeo and Jen are shopping for old things.

___ **2** School wasn't very important for Tadeo.

___ **3** Tadeo's teacher was good.

B 🔊 11.01 LISTEN FOR SUPPORTING DETAILS **Listen to the conversation again. What does Tadeo keep? Does he keep it because it's expensive, or because he loves it?**

3 WRITING

A **Read Ichiko's email. Write the correct topic sentences (a–c) for the paragraphs (1–3).**

> a There's a photo of you and me at the airport.
>
> b Do you remember our trip to Colombia in 2010?
>
> c I have a photo of you on the beach.

Reply   Forward   ✉

Hi Rafa,

1 _____

We went to the beach in Santa Marta. We were there day and night because there were no hotels. It was great. It wasn't very expensive, and it was really beautiful. I'm writing to you because I have some pictures from the trip!

2 _____

You're in the water 🌊 next to a really tall man, and you're wearing a new shirt. You were very cute. Do you remember the guy's name? I think he was from Canada. 🇨🇦

3 _____

I'm wearing a long skirt with flowers. 🌸 The flowers on my skirt were red, yellow, and orange. Your shirt was pink and purple. I can't remember your shorts. They weren't very nice. Do you remember them? Do you have the photo? 📷

Love,

Ichiko

B **Read the sentences and check (✓) where emojis are correct.**

1 (At the doctor's office) Can the doctor see me tomorrow? 😲 _____

2 (On social media) I was at work until 10:30 last night. 😠 _____

3 (In a text message) Do you want to get together on the weekend? 😲 _____

4 (At school) Professor Marumi, I'm not going to be in class next week. 😠 _____

C **Write an email about a trip in the past. Use one paragraph for each idea. Write a topic sentence for each paragraph.**

CHECK AND REVIEW

Read the statements. Can you do these things?

	Mark the boxes. ☑ I can do it. [?] I am not sure.	If you are not sure, go back to these pages in the Student's Book.
	I can …	
VOCABULARY	☐ use adjectives to describe people, places, and things.	page 108
	☐ use words for colors.	page 110
GRAMMAR	☐ use statements with *was* and *were*	page 109
	☐ use questions with *was* and *were*	page 111
FUNCTIONAL LANGUAGE	☐ express uncertainty.	page 112
	☐ take time to think.	page 113
SKILLS	☐ use topic sentences in your writing.	page 115
	☐ write an email about an experience in the past.	page 115

12.1 BACKPACKING AND SNACKING

1 VOCABULARY: Snacks and small meals

A **Cross out the word that does <u>not</u> complete each sentence.**

1	I usually drink _____ juice with my breakfast.	apple	pineapple	~~potato~~
2	_____ comes from an animal.	Chicken	Beef	Soup
3	_____ is a dairy product.	Lamb	Cheese	Butter
4	_____ is made from grain.	a cracker	a pineapple	bread
5	_____ are fruit that grow on trees.	Potatoes	Coconuts	Oranges
6	I often have _____ for lunch.	soup	sandwiches	butter
7	I use _____ to make vegetable soup.	tomatoes	potatoes	apples

2 GRAMMAR: Simple past statements

A **Complete the sentences. Write the simple past form of the verbs.**

1 I like apples. I _____liked_____ apples when I was a child.

2 They don't go to the supermarket on Saturday. They _____ to the supermarket last Saturday.

3 Elena tries a different restaurant every month. She _____ a different restaurant last month.

4 We eat bread every day. We _____ bread yesterday.

5 I don't drink tea at night. I _____ tea last night.

6 Max always buys food on Sunday. He _____ food last Sunday.

B   **Change the affirmative (+) verbs so they're negative (−). Change the negative (−) verbs so they're affirmative (+).**

1   I didn't eat beef. I _____ *ate* _____ chicken.

2   I didn't drink coffee. I _____ tea.

3   Ramon liked the Chinese restaurant. He _____ the French restaurant.

4   The bus didn't arrive at 10:15. It _____ at 10:20.

5   We went to the supermarket. We _____ to the park.

6   We didn't stop for lunch. We _____ for a snack.

3   GRAMMAR AND VOCABULARY

A   **Write true affirmative (+) and negative (−) sentences about the past. Use the words in the box or your own ideas.**

apple/apples	butter	cracker/crackers	potato/potatoes
banana/bananas	cheese	lamb	sandwich/sandwiches
beef	chicken	orange/oranges	soup
bread	coconut/coconuts	pineapple/pineapples	tomato/tomatoes

1   I / have / for dinner last night

   I had chicken for dinner last night. I didn't have lamb.

2   I / buy / last week

   _____

3   I / need / yesterday

   _____

4   I / like / when I was a child

   _____

5   I / want / last weekend

   _____

6   I / eat / for breakfast this morning

   _____

1 VOCABULARY: Food, drinks, and desserts

A **Find the words in the box in the word search.**

black beans	chocolate cake
cookies	eggs
fish	green beans
ice cream	juice
pizza	rice
soda	steak
water	

C	F	D	J	U	Z	G	R	Y	Z	K	W	P
O	F	J	A	G	P	R	H	S	O	D	A	L
O	C	O	B	J	R	E	G	Y	U	I	T	V
K	J	T	L	U	Q	E	Y	H	P	F	E	I
I	L	F	G	I	H	N	J	O	P	I	R	C
E	B	L	A	C	K	B	E	A	N	S	C	E
S	A	X	C	E	V	E	B	G	D	H	M	C
Z	D	P	P	I	Y	A	Y	R	G	J	S	R
W	A	A	I	J	K	N	O	Q	W	S	T	E
R	X	D	R	Z	K	S	H	S	A	F	E	A
I	H	B	S	T	Z	A	Z	C	V	R	A	M
C	H	O	C	O	L	A	T	E	C	A	K	E
E	F	U	O	P	T	F	J	E	M	G	K	M

2 GRAMMAR: Simple past questions; *any*

A **Complete the sentences with *some* or *any*.**

1 I didn't have _____ *any* _____ breakfast this morning.

2 Armando wanted _____ cookies last night.

3 Did you eat _____ rice yesterday?

4 We didn't have _____ homework last week.

5 I had _____ juice with my breakfast this morning.

6 Manolo went to the supermarket because he wanted to buy _____ fruit.

7 Were there _____ desserts at lunch?

8 My children didn't drink _____ soda with lunch.

B **Use the words to write questions about the past. Then answer the questions for you.**

1 you / see / your friends / on the weekend

Did you see your friends on the weekend?   No, I didn't. They were working.

2 you and your family / have / dinner at home / last Friday

3 what / you / eat / yesterday

4 how / they / hear / about the new café

5 he / drink / soda / at breakfast

6 you / go / to the movie theatre / after dinner

7 where / she / buy / the pineapples

8 you / take / your friends / to your favorite restaurant / last month

3 GRAMMAR AND VOCABULARY

A **Write questions so the answers are true for you. Use the words in exercise 1A. You can use *any*.**

1 A Did you have any juice yesterday morning?

   B Yes, I did. I had some orange juice.

2 A _____ last week?

   B No, I didn't. I don't like it, so I never drink it.

3 A _____ yesterday afternoon?

   B Yes, I did. I had some with lunch.

4 A _____ yesterday?

   B Yes, I did. I eat some every day.

5 A Where _____?

   B At the supermarket.

6 A How _____?

   B I didn't cook them. I never cook them.

PLEASE PASS THE BUTTER

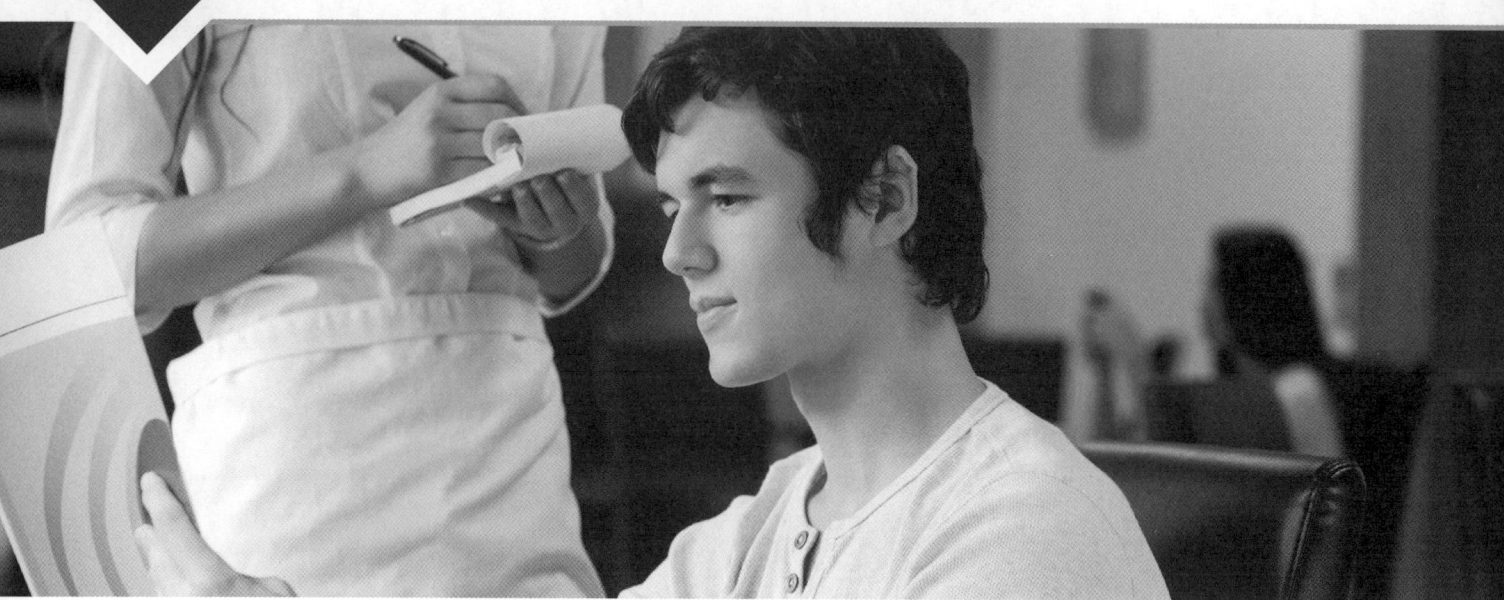

1 FUNCTIONAL LANGUAGE: Making and responding to offers and requests

A **Rewrite the sentences. Use *would like* or *'d like*.**

1 I want some fish, please.   I would like (OR I'd like) some fish, please.
2 Do you want some rice with the fish?
3 What do you want to drink?
4 When do you want the bread?
5 We want a table for six people.
6 Do you want a table near the window?

B **Circle the correct words.**

Server Is everything OK?

Endo ¹I want water. / Can I have some water , please?

Server ²Of course. / Thanks. […] ³Here you are. / This is your food.

Endo Thank you. I ⁴like / 'd like some juice, too. ⁵Do you have / How about orange juice?

Server I'm sorry. ⁶We have / It's orange soda but not orange juice. ⁷Do / Would you like some orange soda?

Endo No, thanks. […] Luis, please ⁸take / pass the bread.

Luis ⁹Here you are. / No, thank you.

Endo Thanks.

2 REAL-WORLD STRATEGY: Using *so* and *really* to make words stronger

A **Add *so* or *really* to the sentences.**

1 This chocolate cake is good.
2 I want to go to the pizza restaurant.
3 My cell phone is cool.
4 Our apartment is small.
5 I need a vacation!

3 FUNCTIONAL LANGUAGE AND REAL-WORLD STRATEGY

A **Sandy is on a plane. Write the missing words in her conversation.**

Jake Would you ¹ _____like_____ something to drink?

Sandy ² _____ you have juice?

Jake We ³ _____ apple juice and orange juice.

Sandy ⁴ _____ I have some apple juice, please?

Jake ⁵ _____ course. And what ⁶ _____ you like for dinner? We ⁷ _____ chicken or fish.

Sandy I'd ⁸ _____ the chicken, please.

Jake Do you ⁹ _____ green beans or black beans with the chicken?

Sandy ¹⁰ _____ like black beans, please.

Jake ¹¹ _____ you are.

Sandy Thank you.

B **Imagine you are on a plane. You are going to eat and drink something. Write a conversation with the server. Say what you would like.**

_____

_____

_____

_____

_____

_____

_____

_____

_____

_____

WHAT DID THE REVIEWERS SAY?

1 LISTENING

A 🔊 **12.01** **LISTEN FOR DETAILS** Listen to Mia and Seb talking about hotels. Which hotel do they choose – Astoria Hotel, Capital Hotel, or White Doors Hotel?

B 🔊 **12.01** **LISTEN FOR SUPPORTING DETAILS** Listen again. Match the hotels (1–3) with the correct information (a–f). You can use some information two times.

1 Astoria Hotel _____
2 Capital Hotel _____
3 White Doors Hotel _____

a It's expensive.
b It's near the ocean.
c It's on a quiet street.
d People need a car for this hotel.
e The reviews of the hotel restaurant are good.
f The hotel always has great reviews.

2 READING

A Read the hotel review. Write (+) next to the things the reviewer liked. Write (–) next to the things the reviewer didn't like. Write (X) next to the things the reviewer did not write about.

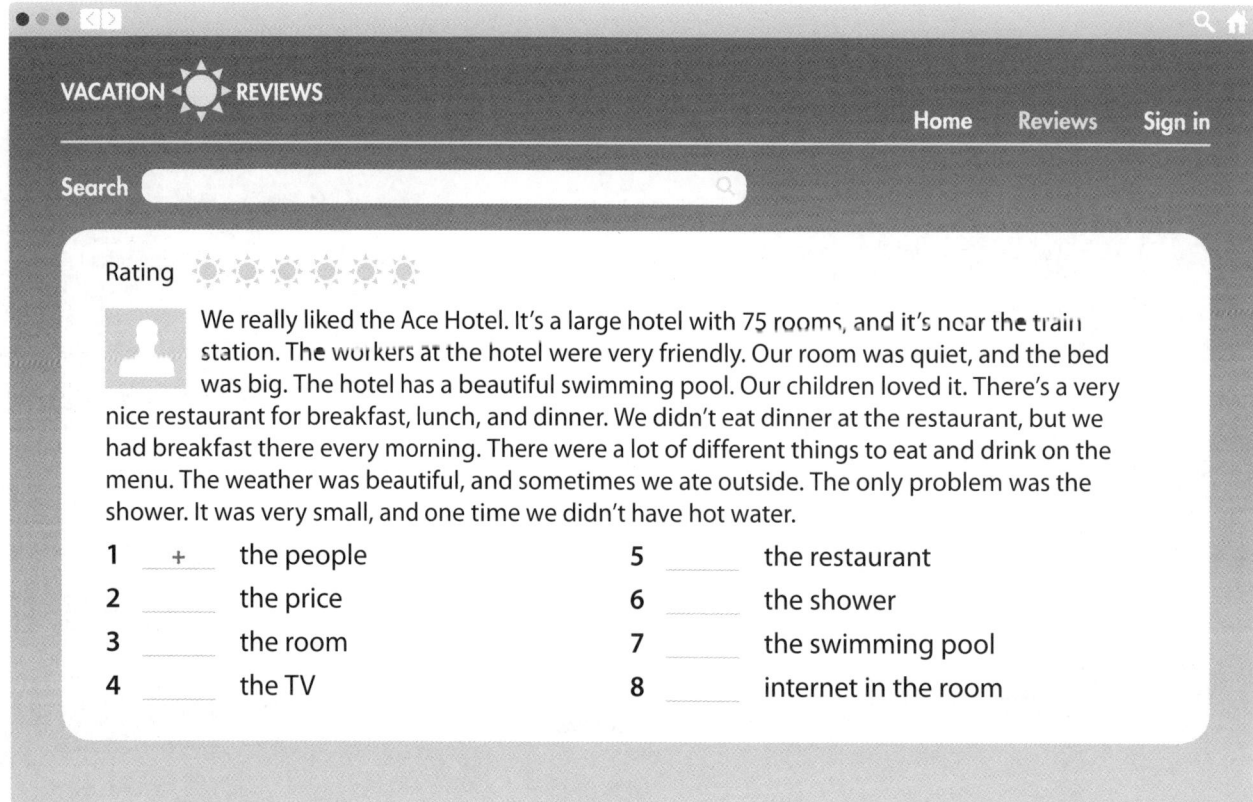

VACATION REVIEWS

Home   Reviews   Sign in

Search 🔍

Rating ☀ ☀ ☀ ☀ ☀ ☀

We really liked the Ace Hotel. It's a large hotel with 75 rooms, and it's near the train station. The workers at the hotel were very friendly. Our room was quiet, and the bed was big. The hotel has a beautiful swimming pool. Our children loved it. There's a very nice restaurant for breakfast, lunch, and dinner. We didn't eat dinner at the restaurant, but we had breakfast there every morning. There were a lot of different things to eat and drink on the menu. The weather was beautiful, and sometimes we ate outside. The only problem was the shower. It was very small, and one time we didn't have hot water.

1 __+__ the people
2 _____ the price
3 _____ the room
4 _____ the TV
5 _____ the restaurant
6 _____ the shower
7 _____ the swimming pool
8 _____ internet in the room

3 WRITING

A **Add commas to the sentences when necessary.**

1 We stayed at the hotel on Monday, Tuesday, and Wednesday.

2 The room was noisy and small.

3 We had lunch and dinner at the hotel.

4 The hotel is near popular restaurants cafés and stores.

5 The busy months at my job are May June and July.

6 I went with my brother my sister and my cousin.

B **Read the questions and answers. Check (✓) when the speaker answers his or her own question.**

1 Where did you stay?   At a hotel near the beach.   _____

2 Am I happy?   Of course, I'm happy.   _____

3 Did I like the chocolate cake?   I loved the chocolate cake!   _____

4 Do you want some pizza?   No, thank you. I'd like a sandwich.   _____

C **Imagine you stayed at a hotel in your town. Write a review of the hotel. Describe the hotel and where it is. Say what is good (or bad) about the hotel.**

CHECK AND REVIEW

Read the statements. Can you do these things?

UNIT 12	Mark the boxes. ✔ I can do it. ? I am not sure. I can …	If you are not sure, go back to these pages in the Student's Book.
VOCABULARY	☐ use words for snacks and small meals. ☐ use words for food, drinks, and desserts.	page 118 page 120
GRAMMAR	☐ use the simple past in statements. ☐ use the simple past in *yes/no* and information questions. ☐ use *any*.	page 119 page 121 page 121
FUNCTIONAL LANGUAGE	☐ offer and request food and drink. ☐ use *so* and *really* to make words stronger.	page 122 page 123
SKILLS	☐ use commas in lists. ☐ write a hotel review.	page 125 page 125

EXTRA ACTIVITIES

7 TIME TO SPEAK Your life these days

A **Look online for books, movies, and songs.**

- What books are people reading these days?
- What movies are people watching these days?
- What songs are people listening to these days?

B **Write sentences and read to your class.**

8 TIME TO SPEAK National skills

A **People in these countries speak English. Choose <u>five</u> countries.**

- Australia
- Canada
- Ireland
- Jamaica
- New Zealand
- South Africa
- the United Kingdom
- the United States

B **Write sentences about what people in each country can do really well.**

C **Read your sentences to your class. Do other students agree?**

9 TIME TO SPEAK Vacation plans

A **Make travel plans.**

- Where do you want to go?
- What do you want to do?
- What do you need to do to travel there?

I want to go to San Diego … I want to swim and go to the zoo. I need to fly from my city.

B **Tell the class about your vacation plans.**

C **Do other students have different ideas?**

10 TIME TO SPEAK 48 hours in your city

A **Imagine a group of college students is going to visit your city next month. Plan 48 hours in your city for the group. Make a list of interesting things they can do in your city.**

B **Read your list to the class. Do you have the same ideas?**

11 TIME TO SPEAK TV memories

A **Talk to your family and friends about their favorite childhood TV shows.**

B **Go online and find information (names, places, things) about the shows.**

C **Write sentences about the shows.**

D **Read your sentences to your class. Did other students write sentences about the same shows?**

12 TIME TO SPEAK Recipe for a great restaurant

A **Look online for a restaurant you want to visit.**

B **Read reviews for the restaurant. What do people like about the restaurant? What do people <u>not</u> like?**

C **Show the restaurant website to the class. Tell the class about the reviewers' comments.**

The authors and publishers acknowledge the following sources of copyright material and are grateful for the permissions granted. While every effort has been made, it has not always been possible to identify the sources of all the material used, or to trace all copyright holders. If any omissions are brought to our notice, we will be happy to include the appropriate acknowledgements on reprinting and in the next update to the digital edition, as applicable.

Key: BL = Below Left, BR = Below Right, CL = Centre Left, T = Top, TR = Top Right.

Photo
All photos are sourced from Getty Images.

p. 50, p. 58 (photo 4), p. 58 (photo 12), p. 74: Westend61; p. 51, p. 85 (girl): Hero Images; p. 52: M_a_y_a/E+; p. 54: DMEPhotography/iStock/ Getty Images Plus; p. 55: Fresh Meat Media LLC/The Image Bank; p. 56: Jim Craigmyle/Corbis; p. 58 (photo 1): Efenzi/E+; p. 58 (photo 2): Ruth Jenkinson/Dorling Kindersley; p. 58 (photo 3): Flyfloor/E+; p. 58 (photo 5): MCCAIG/iStock/Getty Images Plus; p. 58 (photo 6): otnaydur/Shut- terstock; p. 58 (photo 7): Kevin Smith/Perspectives; p. 58 (photo 8): Jerry Driendl/The Image Bank; p. 58 (photo 9): JGI/Blend Images; p. 58 (photo 10): Caiaimage/Sam Edwards/OJO+; p. 58 (photo 11): Jose Luis Pelaez Inc/Blend Images; p.58 (waves): Specker/Vedfelt/Taxi; p. 60: Skynesh- er/E+; p. 61: Monkeybusinessimages/iStock/Getty Images Plus; p. 62: PeopleImages/E+; p. 63: Steve Debenport/iStock/Getty Images Plus; p. 64: Kohei Hara/DigitalVision; p. 66: Tim Boyle/Getty Images; p. 67 (TR): Saro17/E+; p. 67 (CL): RachelDewis/iStock/Getty Images Plus; p. 67 (BR): Jose Fuste Raga/Corbis Documentary; p. 68: Studio 504/Stone; p. 69: Marco Brivio/Photographer's Choice RF; p. 70: Hiya Images/Corbis/ VCG/Corbis; p. 71, p. 92: Andresr/E+; p. 72: GUY Christian/Hemis.fr; p. 75: Troy Aossey/Taxi; p. 76: Seanscott/RooM; p. 77: 97/E+; p. 78: Seb Oliver/Image Source; p. 80 (T): Bjorn Andren; p. 80 (BL): NightAnd- DayImages/E+; p. 80 (BR): Ken Ross/VW Pics/UIG/Getty Images; p. 82: Erik Isakson/Blend Images; p. 83: JTB Photo/UIG/Getty Images; p. 84: Daniele Carotenuto Photography/Moment; p. 85 (shoe): Peter Dazeley/ Photographer's Choice; p. 86: Thomas Barwick/Taxi; p. 87: Luis Alvarez/ Taxi; p. 88: Switch/ailead/amana images; p. 90: GUIZIOU Franck/ hemispicture.com/hemis.fr; p. 91: David Nevala/Aurora; p. 93 (T): Eileen Bach/Iconica; p. 93 (BR): Rosemary Calvert/Photographer's Choice RF; p. 94: Wavebreakmedia/iStock/Getty Images Plus; p. 95: Zoranm/E+; p. 96: LOOK Photography/UpperCut Images.

The following image is from other image library:

p. 58 (photo 6): otnaydur/Shutterstock.

Front cover photography by Arctic-Images/The Image Bank/Getty Images.

Audio production by CityVox, New York.

Corpus
Development of this publication has made use of the Cambridge English Corpus (CEC). The CEC is a multi-billion word collection of contemporary spoken and written English. It includes British English, American English, and other varieties. It also includes the Cambridge Learner Corpus, the world's biggest collection of learner writing, developed in collaboration with Cambridge Assessment. Cambridge University Press uses the CEC to provide evidence about language use that helps to produce better language teaching materials.

Our Evolve authors study the Corpus to see how English is really used, and to identify typical learner mistakes. This information informs the authors' selection of vocabulary, grammar items and Student's Book Corpus features such as the Accuracy Check, Register Check, and Insider English.

IRREGULAR VERBS

Base form	Simple past	Past participle
be	was/were	been
become	became	became
begin	began	begun
break	broke	broken
bring	brought	brought
build	built	built
buy	bought	bought
can	could	-
catch	caught	caught
choose	chose	chosen
come	came	come
cost	cost	cost
cut	cut	cut
do	did	done
draw	drew	drawn
drink	drank	drunk
drive	drove	driven
eat	ate	eaten
fall	fell	fallen
feel	felt	felt
find	found	found
fly	flew	flown
forget	forgot	forgotten
get	got	gotten
give	gave	given
go	went	gone
grow	grew	grown
have	had	had
hear	heard	heard
hit	hit	hit
keep	kept	kept
know	knew	known
leave	left	left
lend	lent	lent

Base form	Simple past	Past participle
lie	lay	lain
lose	lost	lost
make	made	made
mean	meant	meant
meet	met	met
pay	paid	paid
put	put	put
read	read	read
ride	rode	ridden
ring	rang	rung
run	ran	run
say	said	said
see	saw	seen
sell	sold	sold
send	sent	sent
show	showed	shown
sing	sang	sung
sit	sat	sat
sleep	slept	slept
speak	spoke	spoken
spend	spent	spent
stand	stood	stood
swim	swam	swum
take	took	taken
teach	taught	taught
tell	told	told
think	thought	thought
throw	threw	thrown
understand	understood	understood
wake	woke	woken
wear	wore	worn
win	won	won
write	wrote	written

This page is intentionally left blank